FROM PiE TOWN to YuM YuM

Weird and Wacky Place Names Across the United States

BLAND   TASTY   MIXED

Written by Debbie Herman
Illustrated by Linda Sarah Goldman

Kane Miller
A DIVISION OF EDC PUBLISHING

Kane Miller, A Division of EDC Publishing

For information contact:
Kane Miller, A Division of EDC Publishing
PO Box 470663
Tulsa, OK 74147-0663
www.kanemiller.com
www.edcpub.com
www.usbornebooksandmore.com

Library of Congress Control Number: 2011920391

Manufactured by Regent Publishing Services, Hong Kong
Printed April 2011 in ShenZhen, Guangdong, China
1 2 3 4 5 6 7 8 9 10

ISBN: 978-1-935279-79-2

This book is dedicated to my mother, Charlotte Herman,
and my brother, Michael Herman—my 365-days-a-year,
24-hours-a-day editors. Always interested.
Always helpful. Always encouraging.
Always appreciating. Always incredibly talented.

And in memory of my father, Melvin Herman z"l,
and the wonderful family road trips he took us on,
while never failing to "make mileage."

And thanks, Sharon, Mike, and Karen, for all the fun in the back!

Debbie Herman

For Tom

Linda Sarah Goldman

I LIKE YOU

I LIKE YOU TOO!

Wacky Toponyms!

The study of place names is an actual academic discipline, called toponymy, with place names being called toponyms and those who study them, toponymists. Toponymy studies a place name's origins, meanings and use. It takes into account linguistics, geography, history and folklore, and can tell volumes on the personality of a place, region, or even country. After reading this book, you might, for example, get a sense of the free spirit and rambunctiousness of the American frontier. You'll also see that place names developed in many different ways. Some were named for people, geographical features, or in remembrance of an event. Others were named for local taverns or to encourage new settlers. Many came about by mistake!

You've Got Mail

Towns often didn't have a name until they had a post office. As towns grew, residents applied for a post office, which required submitting a place name to postal authorities. Many wacky place names resulted from the townspeople sitting around trying to decide on a community name. Once approved, the name would become the name of the post office and the community. Some towns had names before they applied for a post office, but if another town in the state had the same name, postal authorities would often require them to change it. Duplicate town names could result in lost mail and lost people!

Will the Real Reason Please Stand Up?

Often, the true origin of a place name is unknown. Sometimes there's no record of it, neither written nor oral. Other times, conflicting theories exist, and it's difficult, at times impossible, to determine which is most accurate. This book tries to provide a range of reasons given for a place name, but doesn't claim to have given every one.

No End to the Madness

This book is by no means an exhaustive list of wacky U.S. place names. There's a whole lot more where these came from!

Town? Village? Hamlet?

There are technical differences between a city, town, village, hamlet, and community, and where possible, places are referred to by their accurate labels. Other times, "town" and "community" are used colloquially.

Onward (IN)!
Enough talk. On with the book! I Hope (AR) you enjoy!

Best (TX),
Debbie Herman

STOP OVER

Itching to know how **Scratch Ankle** got its name? There are different versions of the story, but they all include pesky pests and itchy ankles! According to one story, dogs, goats, sheep, and other flea-ridden animals took shelter from bad weather in a space under the community's schoolhouse. The fleas made their way up to the classroom and bit the students' ankles, causing the kids to scratch. So the school became known as the Scratch Ankle School!

As another story goes, horses and cows kept in pens by the railroad attracted biting flies. Every time log trains drove through the town, the crews saw people scratching their ankles. In a third story, neighbors named the community. When people from the next town over passed through, they noticed residents scratching their ankles because of the mosquitoes, and referred to the town as Scratch Ankle.

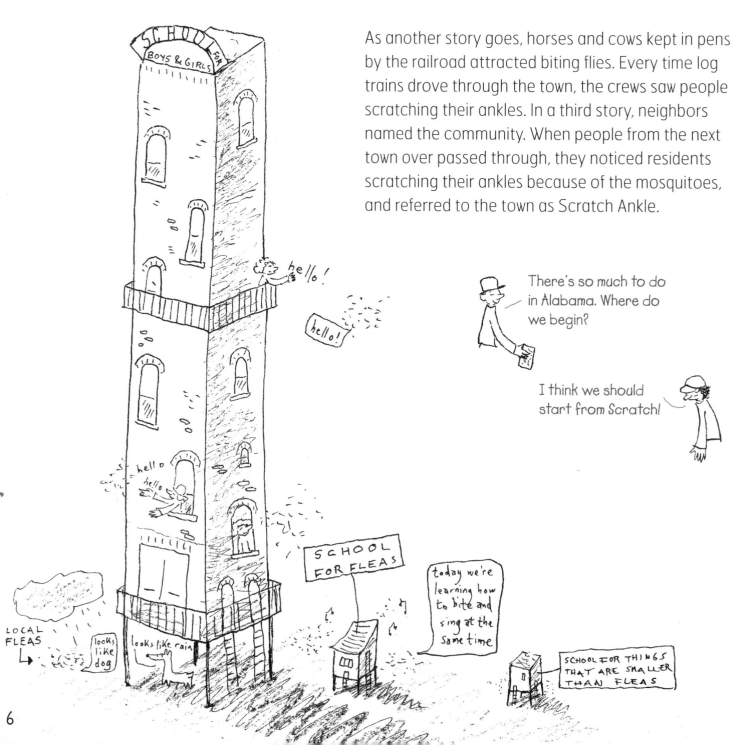

Some Other Wacky Alabama Town Names:

Brilliant	Pull Tight
Bug Tussle	Sardine
Coffeeville	Shorter
Ino	Slapout
Needmore	Taint Much
Pine Apple	Tattlersville
Pronto	Trickem

When residents gathered to name their Alabama town, one person kept saying, "I know what we should call it! I know!" While his suggestions were rejected, his expression was not, and the town was named **Ino**!

Needmore is a common U.S. town name. It usually means the town needs more of everything!

When a country store in the 1920s would run out of an item, its owner would tell the customer, "I'm slap out." So the community came to be known as **Slapout**.

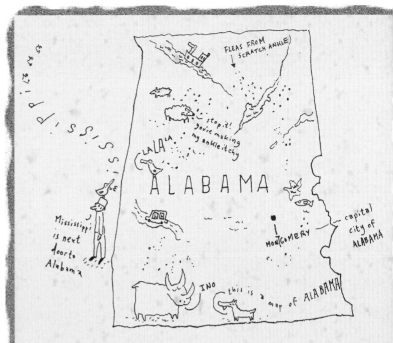

Alabama
Southeastern State
22nd State, Statehood 1819

Info to Know

Monroeville, in Monroe County, Alabama (where Scratch Ankle is located), was home to Harper Lee, author of *To Kill a Mockingbird*. Every May, the Monroe County Heritage Museum performs a play based on the novel. The fame of both the book and the author draws 30,000 tourists to Monroeville each year. A major theme of the book is racial injustice, which the Civil Rights movement of the 1950s and 1960s worked to fight. Alabama was at the center of the Civil Rights movement.

Lay of the Land

Alabama is known for its many underground caves — more than 4,000 of them. You can explore these underground worlds by visiting the many caves open to the public, including DeSoto Caverns, Sequoyah Caverns, and the caverns of the Alabama State Parks.

Road Trip

If you're interested in becoming an astronaut, head out to Huntsville, in northern Alabama, to sign up for Space Camp at the U.S. Space Station and Rocket Center! There you'll experience life on board the International Space Station and feel what it's like to be weightless! The Space and Rocket Center also houses the world's largest space museum. Huntsville has been nicknamed Rocket City because it's home to NASA's Marshall Flight Center which is at the forefront of U.S. space exploration.

COLDFOOT, ALASKA

In 1900, a group of gold seekers traveled up the Koyukuk River to a gold mining town in Alaska's Arctic region, a remote area where winters could be brutal. Once the gold prospectors arrived however, they lost their nerve – got cold feet – and turned right back around! Word got out, and the mining town, then called Slate Creek, was renamed **Coldfoot**!

one of the world's best places to view the Northern Lights

IDITAROD

→ ANCHORAGE

NOME ←

"the last great race on Earth"

There's so much to do near Coldfoot, like explore the Arctic wilderness, or go on a sled dog excursion.

And that's just the tip of the iceberg!

In 1981, Coldfoot became a truck stop – "the farthest north truck stop in the world."

heading north

NORTH STAR

incredibly far north

COLDFOOT TRUCK STOP

CHIP SAND FISH

WILLOW PTARMIGAN

FAIRLY NORTH

QUITE FAR NORTH

EVEN FURTHER NORTH

Some Other Wacky Alaska Town Names:

Candle	North Pole
Chicken	Poorman
Circle	Red Devil
Deadhorse	Saxman
Eek	Sourdough
Farewell	Unalaska
Goodnews Bay	Woodchopper
Igloo	

Chicken was named for the area's many pheasant-like birds — willow ptarmigans — which early miners referred to as chickens. Another explanation is that gold miners once found gold nuggets the size of chicken feed here.

Eek has nothing to do with seeing a mouse! It comes from the Eskimo word *eet*, meaning "two eyes." A nearby creek has the same name. But the reason for the name is unknown.

One explanation behind the name **Unalaska** is that it is derived from *Ounalashka*, the name the Aleut (Unangan) people called it, meaning "near the mainland." Some say it means "this great land."

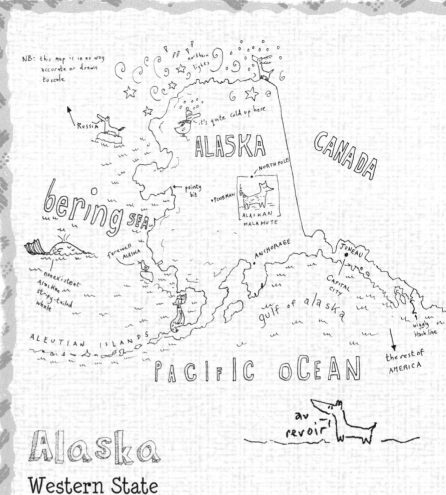

Alaska

Western State
49th State, Statehood 1959

Info to Know

Because of Coldfoot's location in Alaska's far north, it's one of the world's best places to view the Northern Lights!

Lay of the Land

Coldfoot has additional claims to fame: In the 1970s, Coldfoot became a construction camp for workers building the Trans-Alaska Pipeline. The pipeline, which runs through Coldfoot, transports oil from wells in northern Alaska to a port in southern Alaska, where it is loaded onto tankers. The pipeline provides the U.S. with about 6 percent of its oil. In 1981, Coldfoot became a truck stop, dubbed "the farthest north truck stop in the world." Located about halfway between Fairbanks and Prudhoe Bay, it is a convenient stopping point for truck drivers bringing supplies from Fairbanks to oil workers drilling in Prudhoe Bay. Coldfoot is one of the few Alaska communities north of the Arctic Circle that is accessible by road.

Road Trip

The Iditarod Trail Sled Dog Race is a yearly competition. Sled dog drivers, called mushers, race teams of dogs from Anchorage to Nome — a journey of over 1,150 miles. Mushers must battle rough terrain and sub-zero temperatures. One of the most grueling races in the world, the Iditarod is called "the last great race on Earth."

SNOWFLAKE, ARIZONA

When you think of Arizona, you probably picture hot, dry deserts, not icy, cold snowflakes. So why was this town named for the snow crystal? It wasn't! It was named for the town's two founders, Erastus **Snow** and William **Flake**.

Some Other Wacky Arizona Town Names:

Carefree
Chloride
Coffeepot
Grasshopper
Gripe
Happy Jack
Honeymoon
Inspiration

Many Farms
Nothing
Smoke Signal
Surprise
Tombstone
Tortilla Flat
Why

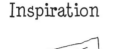

There are different stories behind the origin of **Surprise**. As one story tells it, an early settler said she'd be surprised if the small community ever became a town. Well, surprise, surprise! It's now a city, with more than 100,000 residents! In fact, it's one of the fastest growing communities in the United States!

In 1877, when Ed Schieffelin decided to mine for silver in Apache territory, people thought he was crazy! They told him he would find nothing but his own tombstone. Not only was Schieffelin unharmed, he succeeded in finding silver. Jokingly, he named his first mining claim, **Tombstone**! The town that sprung up in the area took on this name.

Some say **Why** got its name because people used to ask why anyone would want to live there! According to another explanation, it was named for a Y-shaped intersection formed by two major highways.

There used to be towns called **American Flag**, **Big Bug**, **Bumble Bee**, **Pick Em Up** and **Total Wreck**! They are now ghost towns.

Arizona

Southwestern State
48th State, Statehood 1912

Info to Know

It actually does snow in Arizona. Arizona's climate varies from region to region. Southern Arizona has hot, dry summers and mild winters. But the mountainous areas of central and northern Arizona have much cooler summers and very cold winters. These areas can get lots of snow. Some places even have ski resorts. And if you're wondering about Snowflake — it has snowflakes! Located in north central Arizona, Snowflake gets a small amount of quick-melting snow during the winter months.

Lay of the Land

Snowflake is only about a 40-minute drive from Petrified Forest National Park. Once a forested swamp, its trees were buried by sediment and after many years became petrified, turning into fossils as hard as rocks! While you can find petrified wood in other parts of Arizona, Petrified Forest National Park is one of the best places to see these multicolored stone logs.

Road Trip

In Petrified Forest National Park you will find the Painted Desert, hundreds of miles of sandstone formations with beautiful bands of color. The Painted Desert stretches all the way to the Grand Canyon. The Grand Canyon is a magnificent canyon in Arizona that was carved out by the Colorado River. Its many colored layers help us learn how the Earth was formed. The Grand Canyon is 277 miles long, up to 18 miles wide in parts, and more than a mile deep. People come from all over the world to see its spectacular views!

Many different stories have been penned about the origin of **Ink**! One legend has it that Ink got its name by mistake! When this small hamlet was ready for a post office in 1887, it had to decide on a post office name. To do this, forms were given out to its residents. On the form was a blank line to write in a suggested place name. Next to the line were the instructions, "Write in ink." Many residents took these instructions literally and wrote the word *ink* on the line! With the majority of people writing in *ink*, Ink became the official name of the post office and the community! Others explain that in the 1800s, the postmaster of the community sent in his choice for a community name to the U.S. Postal Service. He also sent a list of alternate choices. Ink had actually been his second choice. His first choice had been Melon! Another twist on the story is that the postmaster's wife created the list of names. After staring at a bottle of ink, she decided on Inky. But there already was an Inky in Arkansas, so the U.S. Postal Service changed the name to Ink.

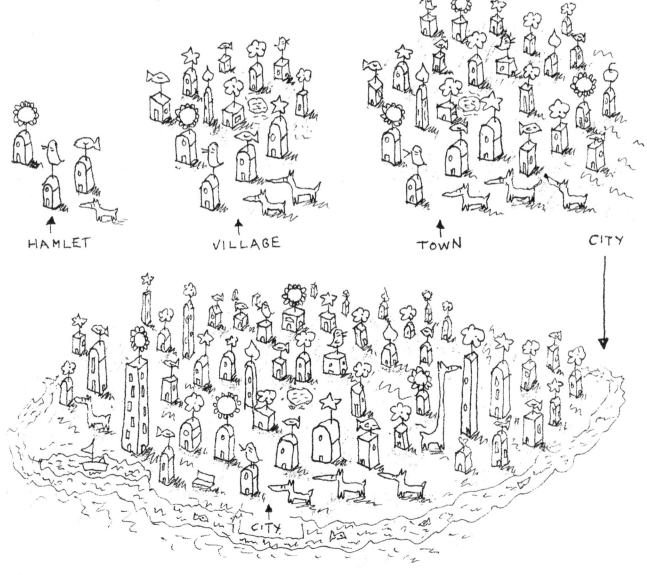

HAMLET   VILLAGE   TOWN   CITY

CITY

Some Other Wacky Arkansas Town Names:

Big Fork	Republican
Catcher	Smackover
Democrat	Stinking Bay
Greasy Corner	Sweet Home
Jumbo	Tomato
Nuckles	Umpire
Ozone	Welcome
Parkin	Yellville

VERY LOUD

LA LA LA LA OOOFFF

YELLVILLE

Smackover is an American mispronunciation of the French name *Sumac Couvert*, which means "sumac-covered." The area was covered with sumac trees.

The town of **Yellville** does not have loud residents. It was named for Arkansas Governor Archibald Yell, who fought in the War of 1812.

Umpire got its name in the 1890s, after the community decided to host a baseball game against a neighboring community. But baseball was a new sport back then, and neither town knew how to play. Luckily, a visitor who *did* know how to play was in town. He acted as umpire and explained the rules. Everyone had a great time, and the residents named their town after this event. Interestingly, not only is there an Umpire, Arkansas, but there's also a **Catcher**, Arkansas!

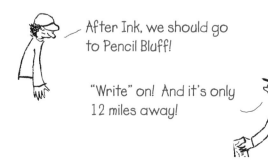

After Ink, we should go to Pencil Bluff!

"Write" on! And it's only 12 miles away!

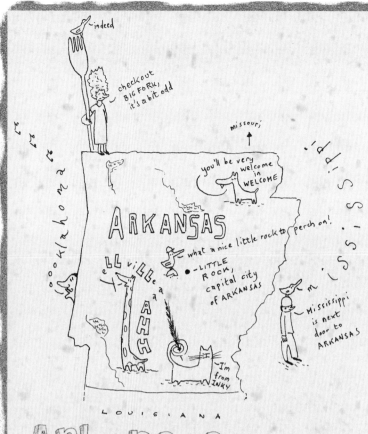

–indeed

check out BIG FORK, it's a bit odd

missouri ↑

you'll be very welcome in WELCOME

ARKANSAS

what a nice little rock to perch on!

• LITTLE ROCK, capital city of ARKANSAS

mississippi is next door to ARKANSAS

ll ville a AHH

–I'm from INKY

oklahoma

LOUISIANA

Arkansas

Southeastern State
22nd State, Statehood 1836

Info to Know

A hamlet is generally smaller than a village (usually having less than 500 people), a village is smaller than a town, and a town is smaller than a city.

Lay of the Land

You may have heard of the Ozarks, an area of low mountains extending through north central and northwest Arkansas, southern Missouri, and parts of Oklahoma and Kansas. The Ozarks have steep slopes and valleys, forests, streams, and even caves! In the Ozark National Forest you'll find Blanchard Springs Caverns, a three-level cave system with stalactites – mineral formulations that hang from the ceiling like icicles – and stalagmites – mineral formations that rise from the cavern floor.

Road Trip

In Crater of Diamonds State Park, in southwest Arkansas, you can dig for diamonds! An ancient volcanic pipe once brought diamonds to the surface of the diamond search area (a 3.75-acre field). Crater of Diamonds is the only diamond-producing site in the world where visitors can actually search for diamonds and keep them!

TARZANA, CALIFORNIA

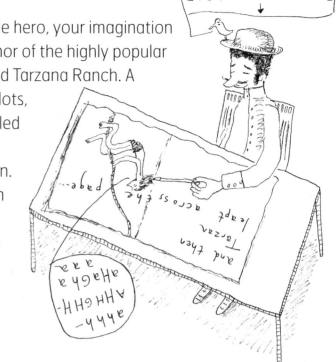

EDGAR RICE BURROUGHS ↓

If **Tarzana** conjures up images of a tree-swinging jungle hero, your imagination is not running wild! In 1919, Edgar Rice Burroughs, author of the highly popular *Tarzan* books, lived in California on an estate he named Tarzana Ranch. A few years later, he divided up a portion of his ranch into plots, for people to buy and build homes on. In 1922, a town called Runnymede was founded next to the Tarzana Ranch. As Runnymede grew, Tarzana Ranch became part of the town. When Runnymede residents petitioned for a post office in 1928, they were told their town name was already taken. To choose a new one, they held a contest. The winner was Tarzana, honoring Burroughs and his jungle adventurer!

Me say it's time to leave Tarzana.

But I was just getting into the swing of things!

Some Other Wacky California Town Names:

Bummerville	Likely
Cheeseville	Needles
Eureka	Ono
Fiddletown	Rough and Ready
Giant	You Bet
Happy Camp	Zzyzx
Igo	

Eureka, meaning "I found it!" in Greek, was so named in 1850 for the cry of gold miners striking gold. Thousands of immigrants rushed to California to discover gold between 1848 and 1859, in what became known as the California Gold Rush. The gold rush was at its peak in 1849, which is why miners were often referred to as '49ers.

The city of **Needles**, in the Mohave Valley, was named for a group of pointed peaks called *The Needles*, at the valley's southern end. The Mohave Valley straddles the California-Arizona border.

Zzyzx is pronounced ZYE-ziks. The name was made up by the man who built the settlement, in 1944, which included a mineral springs, health spa, and radio station. He chose the name because he wanted it to be the last word in the dictionary! The land didn't actually belong to him, however. It belonged to the Federal Government! In 1974, the government took back the land and eventually replaced the spa with a research center.

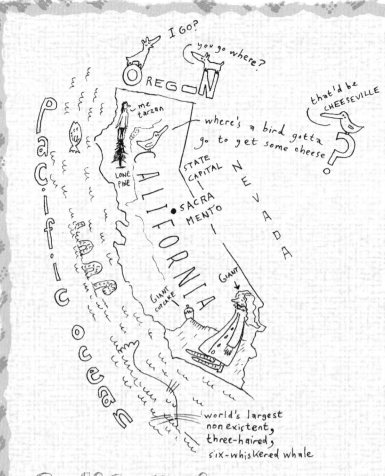

California

Western State
31st State, Statehood 1850

Info to Know

The town of Tarzan, Texas, was also named for Burroughs' fictional character. Postal officials chose Tarzan out of the 14 town names suggested. They must have been fans of the Ape Man too!

Lay of the Land

Tarzana is a district of Los Angeles, located in the San Fernando Valley, in the foothills of the beautiful Santa Monica Mountains. People often refer to the San Fernando Valley as *The Valley*. Tarzana is one of the Valley's oldest communities.

Road Trip

Visit Yosemite National Park, one of the country's first wilderness parks, especially known for its waterfalls. Yosemite Falls is the highest waterfall in the United States. At 2,425 feet, it's much taller than the tallest building in the United States – the Willis Tower, in Chicago, Illinois – which is "only" 1,451 feet! Travel along the rugged terrain of Yosemite from on top of a mule! Mule riding is an excellent and unique way to explore Yosemite National Park, and experience its breathtaking views!

Here comes **Troublesome**! This town took its name from a creek in the area that had thick mud at the bottom. The mud made it troublesome for wagons trying to cross the creek, which is how it earned the name Troublesome Creek. Some say the creek was named in the 1860s, when a U.S. Cavalry unit had trouble crossing it.

So many huge, snow-covered mountains

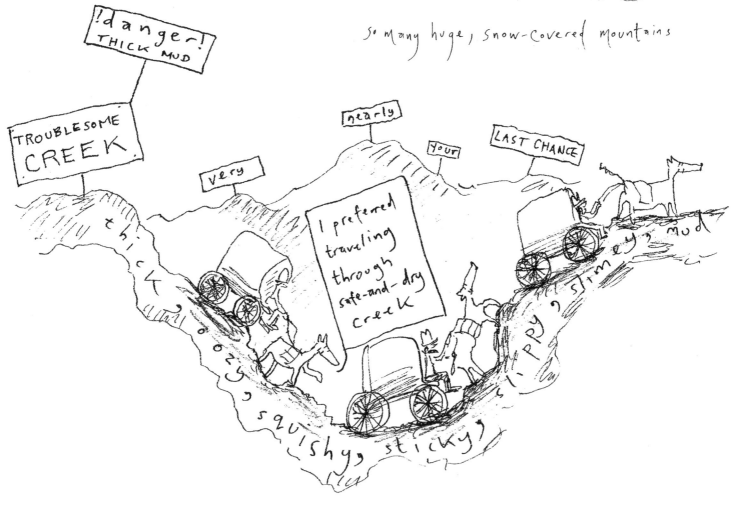

I want to ski, snowboard, hike, mountain climb, bathe in the hot springs...

Now you're just being troublesome!

Some Other Wacky Colorado Town Names:

Crook	Parachute
Goodnight	Paradox
Hasty	Rush
Hygiene	Spook City
Joes	Tin Cup
Last Chance	Toonerville
No Name	Wide Awake

THREE JOES AND ONE GIRAFFE

Last Chance, located about 65 miles east of Denver, got its name because it was the last chance to get gasoline for miles.

Some simply state that **No Name** was named for No Name Creek and No Name Canyon. Others explain that when Interstate 70 was completed, the Colorado Department of Transportation put up highway signs. One area had no name, so on the sign for Exit 119 – the exit leading to the area – officials wrote "No Name." Residents got so used to it, when officials gave the place a "proper" name, they fought to have it changed back!

The village of **Joes**, originally called Three Joes, was named for three early settlers named Joe.

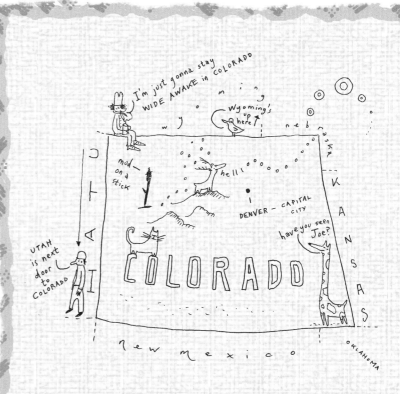

Colorado

Western State
38th State, Statehood 1876

Info to Know

Not far from Troublesome is the town of Hot Sulphur Springs, where people come to bathe and relax in its hot springs – natural springs that produce hot water. Hot Sulphur Springs is just one of the many places you'll find hot springs in Colorado.

Lay of the Land

After visiting Hot Sulphur Springs, you can move on to Rocky Mountain National Park. There you'll find the breathtaking mountains and peaks of the Rocky Mountains. The Rocky Mountains are a major mountain range in western North America. The Rockies, as they're often called, stretch from northern Mexico to northwest Alaska. The highest peak is Mount Elbert, in Colorado!

Road Trip

Colorado has so many huge, snow-covered mountains, people come from all over to enjoy some of the best skiing and snowboarding in the country! Visit Vale Mountain, the largest single mountain ski resort in the United States, located high in the Colorado Rockies! The area has great summer activities too, such as rafting, jeep tours, horseback riding, and hot air ballooning!

HATTERTOWN, CONNECTICUT

I f you're looking for the Mad Hatter, you won't find him here in **Hattertown**, though this community was named for a hatter, or hat maker, in the early 1800s. Elam Benedict started a hat-making business in this community with his business partner, Levi Taylor. They decided it was a good place to set up shop because there were no other hatters in the area, and the streams were filled with beaver and muskrat, animals whose fur was used in making hats. But other hatters did eventually start working here, and by 1846 there were seven hat factories in town. At least Benedict and Taylor had a head start!

Where should we head to after Hattertown?

Whigville!

18

Some Other Wacky Connecticut Town Names:

Bakersville	Plainville
Banksville	Plantsville
Derby	Upper Merryall
Giants Neck	(and Lower Merryall)
Mechanicsville	Voluntown
Mystic	Whigville
Orange	Woodtick

Mystic is not a mystical town. The name is derived from an Algonquian word meaning "Great tidal river." *Mystic* was first applied to a stream, and then to the village. It was also applied to other features and places in the area.

In the 1700s, land surveyors were surveying a piece of land in Milford, Connecticut. When stopping for the night, they started drinking and they "all became merry." That's how **Upper Merryall** and **Lower Merryall** got their names. This is one of only a few cases where a New England community was named for a frivolous, or silly, reason.

If you thought **Voluntown** had something to do with volunteering, then you thought right! The land, originally called Volunteer Town, was given to settlers who volunteered to fight in King Philip's War, a war between American Indians and English settlers in the years 1675-1676.

Connecticut

Northeastern State
5th State, Statehood 1788

Info to Know

Sadly, Benedict and Taylor both died at an early age, probably from mercury poisoning. In those days, mercury, a poisonous metallic element, was used in the hat-making process. It caused many hatters to suffer nerve damage, making them tremble, slur their speech, and exhibit behaviors that made people think they'd gone mad. Some say this is the origin of the phrase "mad as a hatter."

Lay of the Land

Northeast of Hattertown is central Connecticut's Hartford County, where there's lots to do! In Plainville, watch balloon-filled skies during the spectacular Hot Air Balloon Festival. Visit the many museums of Bristol, such as the American Clock and Watch Museum and the New England Carousel Museum. At the Farmington Historical Society in Farmington you can tour the Freedom Trail's Underground Railroad and Amistad sites. The Underground Railroad was a network of secret routes and safe houses used by slaves to escape to the free states of the North. *Amistad* was a slave ship on which a slave rebellion took place.

Road Trip

Another great place to visit east of Hattertown is Hamden, Connecticut, home to the Eli Whitney Museum, where kids blend science and invention through designing and building their own creations! The museum also teaches about Eli Whitney, the famous American inventor best known for his invention of the cotton gin, and A.C. Gilbert, inventor and toy maker, best known for his invention of the Erector Set.

MERMAID, DELAWARE

Sorry, no mythological sea creatures here! The Mermaid Tavern, built around 1746, was a stagecoach stop. But over time it became more than just a place for weary travelers to lay their heads or have a drink. It became a hangout for locals and a full-service station for stagecoaches and wagons, with horse stables, a blacksmith and a wheelwright — the auto mechanic of the olden days — housed nearby. As a single-street village grew up around the tavern, it was naturally called **Mermaid**. And that's no fish tale!

GET YOUR WHEELS FIXED HERE

MERMAID TAVERN

1746 (approx.)

something fishy HOTEL

WELCOME TO MERMAID

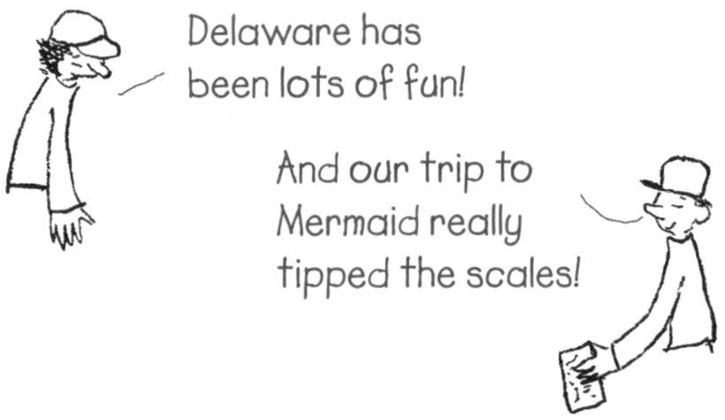

Delaware has been lots of fun!

And our trip to Mermaid really tipped the scales!

WILMINGTON →

ALL ABOARD!

DELAWARE 1ST STATE

HOWDY

Chugging through Delaware's historic and scenic RED CLAY CREEK VALLEY!

Some Other Wacky Delaware Town Names:

Bear
Blackbird
Blades
Cannon
Cocked Hat
Great Good Place
Hardscrabble

Hourglass
Pepper
Red Lion
Rising Sun
Stones Throw
Viola

According to legend, the town of **Blackbird** was originally called Blackbeard, for the greatly feared pirate of the early 1700s. Later, residents wanted to change the name of their town, without making it too different. Lucky for them, the area had many blackbirds, so the switch was easy. *Blackbeard* became *Blackbird*! Others say Blackbird was simply named for the local Black Birds Creek, or for the large flocks of blackbirds.

Hardscrabble has nothing to do with word games. Hardscrabble was a term used to describe a very poor town, or one with such poor soil, farmers could barely make a living from it. Either or both of these definitions could explain how this town got its unfortunate name.

As one story tells it, the town of **Rising Sun**, like many places in early America, was named for a tavern of the same name.

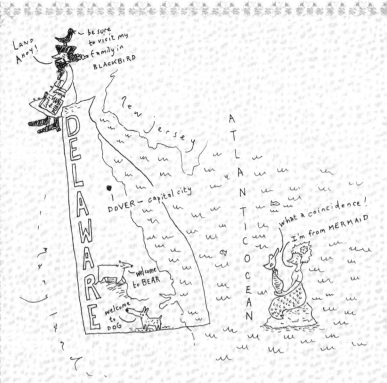

Delaware

Northeastern State
1st State, Statehood 1787

Info to Know

The Mermaid Tavern also served as a post office and polling station (a place for people to vote). The Mermaid still stands today and is on the National Register of Historic Places, an official list of historic sites in the United States that are worthy of preservation.

Lay of the Land

About five miles northeast of Mermaid, in northern Delaware, is Mount Cuba Center, which has about 600 acres of forests, wetlands, and open fields. There you can enjoy guided tours of beautiful gardens filled with shrubs, trees, and wildflowers. Another place to visit is nearby Hockessin, home to the Ashland Nature Center, where you can walk along trails winding through meadows, woodlands and marshes.

Road Trip

Travel back in time! Visit the Wilmington & Western Railroad, from the late 1800s, about 10 miles east of Mermaid, just outside Wilmington. Climb aboard Steam Engine #98, an authentic coal-burning train from 1909. You'll hear the conductor shout, "All aboard!" as he sounds the locomotive's clanging bell. And before you know it, you'll be chugging through Delaware's historic and scenic Red Clay Creek Valley! One railroad line will take you to a picnic area on the property of Mount Cuba Center, and the other will take you to Hockessin.

TWO EGG, FLORIDA

How ~~eggsactly~~ exactly did this town get its name? Details of the story vary, but the basic idea is this: People in the area would sometimes barter, or trade goods, instead of using money to buy things. Eggs were often used for trading, so someone might ask for two eggs worth of sugar. As one story goes, a poor man gave each of his two children a chicken. The children often went to the general store to trade two of the chicken eggs for candy. A traveler witnessed this exchange and referred to the town as *Two-Egg Crossing*. The name caught on and was eventually shortened to **Two Egg**.

Some Other Wacky Florida Town Names:

Celebration	Perky
Corkscrew	Picnic
Doctor Philips	Sawdust
Frostproof	Sopchoppy
Hero	Spuds
Kissimmee	Tangerine
Mayo	Yeehaw Junction
Niceville	

Residents thought their town was a nice place to live, so they called it **Niceville**.

Tangerine, named for the citrus fruit, is appropriately located in Orange County!

As one story tells it, during the Civil War, the Southern military raised donkeys to haul heavy loads of military equipment (some say they hauled trees from nearby forests). The biggest donkey farm was on an area of land in central Florida. After enduring hours of yee-haw-ing donkeys, it was no wonder residents named their town **Yeehaw Junction**. Another reason given for the name is that *Yeehaw* is derived from the Muskogee Creek word meaning "wolf" because of the many wolves in the area.

and everyone was having so much fun, some of the houses in Celebration began floating up, up and away...

Florida
Southeastern State
27th State, Statehood 1845

Info to Know
On the southern tip of Florida are the famous Florida Everglades, a subtropical swamp area known for its wildlife, especially alligators and crocodiles. In fact, it's the only place in the world where alligators and crocodiles exist side by side. The Everglades is home to many rare and endangered species, like the Leatherback Turtle and the Florida Panther.

Lay of the Land
Most of Florida is a peninsula, an area of land surrounded by water on three sides. Two Egg is located in Florida's northwest, often referred to as the Florida Panhandle. A panhandle is a narrow strip of land sticking out from a larger area, like the handle of a pan. Other states with panhandles include Alaska, Idaho, Nebraska, Oklahoma, and Texas.

Road Trip
Visit Florida's Space Coast, a region on the Atlantic Coast, where you can spend time on the beach and exploring space! The Space Coast is home to the Kennedy Space Center and Cape Canaveral, sites of manned and unmanned space launches! At the Kennedy Space Center Visitor Complex, you can learn about the past, present and future of America's space program. Experience a simulated rocket launch, meet an astronaut, view giant rockets, launch sites and maybe even a launch!

BETWEEN, GEORGIA

This town in Walton County got its name because of its location – halfway *between* the cities of Monroe and Loganville! But some tell a more elaborate story: Around the 1850s, people began settling in an area 6 miles west of Monroe and 6 miles east of Loganville. Once or twice a week, someone from Monroe would come to the community to deliver the mail. As the community grew, residents applied for a post office of their own, but each place name they suggested was rejected, and they turned to the postmistress of Monroe for help. One day, the postmistress' husband, fed up with all this town-name talk, told his wife that since the community was between Monroe and Loganville, she should just call it **Between**! She did, and postal authorities accepted the name. It was, after all, the only Between in the state. And even if there were others, I'm sure they were few and far between!

Some Other Wacky Georgia Town Names:

Doctortown	Poetry
Experiment	Saw Dust
Flintstone	Snapfinger
Hopeful	Trickum
Jolly	Veribest
Jot Em Down Store	Wahoo
Little Hope	Welcome
Nameless	

Experiment got its name because it's home to the Georgia Agricultural Experiment Station, which helps develop modern agriculture in the South.

After postal authorities rejected all the suggested names for their community, residents decided their hamlet would be **Nameless**!

Flintstone has nothing to do with cartoon characters! Many arrowheads, tools, and weapons made out of flint, a kind of stone, were found in this area.

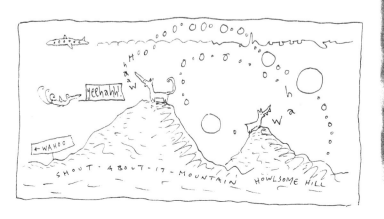

Georgia

Southeastern State
4th State, Statehood 1836

Info to Know

Between is also between two of Georgia's major cities, Athens and Atlanta – the most populated city in Georgia. Atlanta is home to many sites and attractions, including the Georgia Aquarium, the biggest aquarium in the world!

Lay of the Land

In the southeast corner of Georgia is the Okefenokee Swamp. American Indians called it *Okefenoka*, meaning "land of the trembling earth." At 730 square miles, the Okefenokee is home to more than 400 species of animals. There are alligators, red-cockaded woodpeckers, blue herons and sandhill cranes. The swamp is crisscrossed with miles of water trails for motorboats, canoes and paddle boats.

Road Trip

About 25 miles west of Between is Stone Mountain, one of the world's largest pieces of exposed granite. On the rock is a carving of three Confederate leaders, Jefferson Davis, Thomas Jonathan "Stonewall" Jackson, and Robert E. Lee, who helped lead the South during the Civil War. A cable car takes you to the top of Stone Mountain, showing you a close-up view of the carving along the way!

HAIKU, HAWAII

Haiku is not just the Japanese poetry you learned about in school. It's also a town in the northern part of Maui. The name has been translated in different ways, including "to speak abruptly," "haughty or conceited," and "sharp break." What's the story behind the name? Many experts couldn't even tell you. But looking at the area's beauty, with its waterfalls, rainbows, sugarcane, and tropical landscapes, you're sure to agree that a picture is worth a thousand words!

the Hawaiian alphabet has only twelve letters!

a e i o u h K L M N P W

I think we should go explore Haiku!

You have a way with words!

Some Other Wacky Hawaii Place Names:

Alabama Village
Awaawapuhi
Captain Cook
Crater
Diamond Head
Happy Valley
Papa
Pearl City
Pepeekeo
Pepeiaolepo
Volcano
Waiakea
Waimea

Awaawapuhi, a valley and trail on Kauai, means "eel valley," with *puhi* meaning "freshwater eel." A folktale tells how an eel named Kuna was swimming along the cliffs. After some time, he slithered up the cliffs, carving out a valley in the process. Then he fell asleep. Kuna awoke to a group of people who, thinking he was dead, tried to cook him. He ate them instead!

Captain Cook, a town on Hawaii, should not to be confused with Captain Hook of *Peter Pan* fame. Captain Cook was named for Captain James Cook, a British explorer who (along with his two crew members) was the first European to reach the Hawaiian Islands. He was killed in this area, at Kealakekua Bay, in 1779.

Diamond Head, a volcanic crater on Oahu, got its name in the early 1800s, when British soldiers saw calcite crystals in the lava rock and thought they were diamonds. Its original name was *Laeahi*, meaning "brow of the tuna"!

Papa has nothing to do with your father! It is a village on Hawaii and means "forbidden."

Pearl City, on Oahu, was so named because it's located on the shores of Pearl Harbor. "Pearl Harbor" comes from the Hawaiian name *Wai Momi*, meaning "pearl waters," which was named for the pearl-making oysters in the area.

Pepeekeo, a village on Hawaii, means "the food crushed," as by warriors in battle.

Pepeiaolepo, a land division on Maui, means "dirty ear." As the folktale goes, Kama-puaa, who was half man and half hog, got mud in his ear while diving in a stream in the area.

Waiakea, a village on Hawaii, means "broad waters." According to a folktale, during a time of famine, a man who lived in the area, named *Ulu* – meaning "breadfruit"– died of starvation. By the next morning, a breadfruit tree had grown there, ending the famine.

Waimea, a village on Hawaii, means "reddish water," because of the erosion of red soil.

Hawaii

Western State
50th State, Statehood 1959

Info to Know

Hawaiian place names are unlike place names of other states. That's because most places in Hawaii have Hawaiian names, like *Waiohinu* and *Kalaupapa*, meaning "shiny water" and "the flat plain." Some places were named for features in nature, others for people or events. Some now have English names. Many Hawaiian place names are so ancient, the reasons behind them have been lost.

Not only did Hawaiians name their cities and villages, they named everything from rocks, trees, and tiny valleys, to houses, surfing areas, and places where miraculous events are believed to have occurred. Numerous folktales have been passed down that tell mythical stories about a particular place or its name.

The Hawaiian alphabet has only 12 letters! This includes vowels A, E, I, O, U, and the consonants H, K, L, M, N, P, W. There is also the okina symbol, which looks like an upside-down apostrophe: '. The okina is a glottal stop — or brief break in a word — which is similar to the sound between *oh*s in the English "oh-oh." (The correct way to write *Hawaii* is actually "Hawai'i," with an okina.) As you read Hawaiian words and place names, you'll notice that they're made up of these letters.

Lay of the Land

Hawaii is made up of islands. In fact, it is a chain of over 130 islands in the north central Pacific Ocean. Its eight major islands are Hawaii, called the Big Island, Maui, Kahoolawe, Lanai, Molokai, Oahu, Kauai, and Niihau. The state of Hawaii got its name from the island of Hawaii.

Road Trip

While visiting Haiku, near Maui's tropical rainforest, be sure to make your way to nearby Hookipa Beach Park, known for having the world's best windsurfing. Some visitors take helicopter rides over nearby Peahi Beach, nicknamed Jaws, where expert surfers take on waves up to 60 feet high!

Drive the winding Haleakala Crater Road, in East Maui, up to the summit of Haleakala, the tallest volcano on Maui, and you'll actually drive through the clouds! Once at the top (10,023 feet), you'll witness an enormous crater, seven miles across, two miles wide, and 3,000 feet deep! Its surroundings, including the cinder cones inside it, will make you feel as if you're on the moon! Make sure to catch a sunrise or sunset on Haleakala. It's an unforgettable site!

After seeing a dormant volcano, how about seeing an active one? Head to Hawaii Volcanoes National Park, on the Big Island, and there's a good chance you'll see red-hot lava ooze from the volcano Kilauea! You'll also see steam vents spewing steam, and huge lava craters, and you'll get to walk through lava tubes! The park also has a tropical rain forest, ancient Hawaiian petroglyphs, and amazing hiking and views!

you'll actually drive through the clouds

CHILLY, IDAHO

Legend has it that when this community was being planned, its founders sat around the fire one cold, cold night, trying to think of a town name. Inspiration hit when someone commented on how chilly it was outside. So **Chilly** it became. Now that's pretty cool!

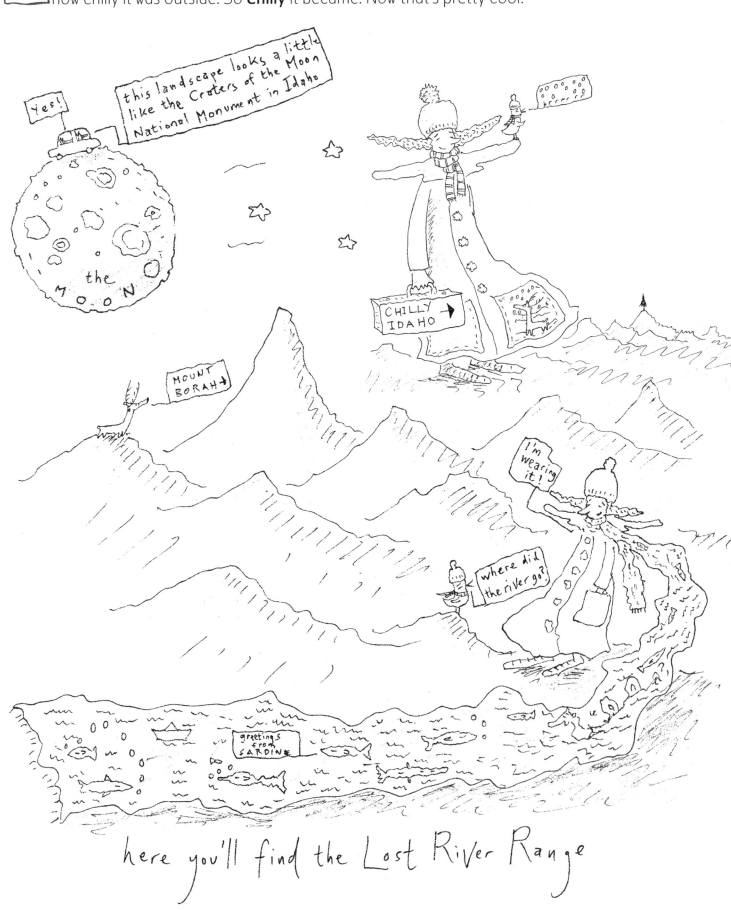

here you'll find the Lost River Range

Some Other Wacky Idaho Town Names:

Arrow
Bench
Bliss
Bone
Culdesac
Dent
Good Grief
Gross
Headquarters
Moody
Riddle
Squirrel
Triangle

Arrow was named for the many arrowheads discovered in the area.

Squirrel was named for all the squirrels found there.

As one story tells it, in the 1950s, a tavern was built in a community in northern Idaho. Its owners named the tavern **Good Grief**, because of a beer deliveryman who'd say "Good grief!" every time he walked through the door. The name caught on, and residents started calling the community Good Grief!

Craters of the Moon was so cool and weird, it gave me goose bumps!

Really? I would have thought you'd get goose bumps in Chilly!

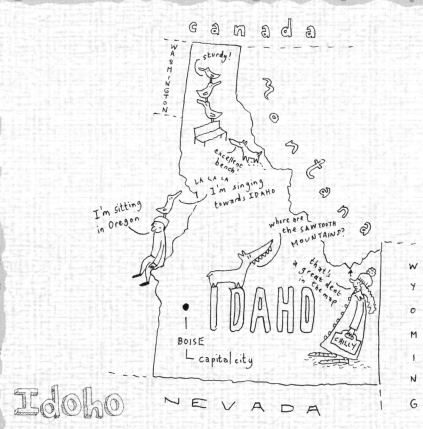

Idaho

Western State
43rd State, Statehood 1890

Info to Know

If you're a rock collector, Idaho is the state for you! It's filled with beautiful precious and semi-precious gems. In the southern part of the state you'll find gems such as agate, opal, and jasper, while in the northern part of the state you'll find diamonds, garnets, and rubies. Some of Idaho's gems are very rare. You can mine for gems in the Spencer Opal Mine in Spencer, Idaho, known as the "Opal Capital of America."

Lay of the Land

Custer County, located in central Idaho, is known for its rugged mountains. Here you'll find the Lost River Range, a mountain range that includes Mount Borah, the highest peak in the state. Also running through Custer County are the famous Sawtooth Mountains, which are part of the Rocky Mountain Range. In the Sawtooth Mountains you can do everything from whitewater rafting and skiing to fly fishing, mountain biking, and rock climbing!

Road Trip

For an out of this world experience, visit Craters of the Moon National Monument, an enormous and extremely weird-looking field of lava formations and volcanoes. Hot lava once oozed and shot out of the earth here and froze in the coolest shapes, twisty tubes, blobs, mounds, and jagged chunks. The volcanoes look like cones and craters. This strange landscape makes visitors feel like they're walking on the moon! And ironically, the lava formations can be seen from space!

DISCO, ILLINOIS

I won't give you a whole song and dance about how this community got its name. The story is simple, and it has nothing to do with the popular music of the 1970s. The community was probably named **Disco** because of where it's located, in a *discus*-shaped valley. (And not under a disco ball!)

are you heading down to DISCO later?

maybe - I do feel like dancing

DISCO

LOUIS JOLIET THE EXPLORER

WELCOME TO JOLIET

Now that we've been to Disco, Illinois, we should head over to Rock, Wisconsin!

Or Waltz, Michigan!

ROMEOVILLE, ROMEOVILLE, Where art thou, my ROMEOVILLE?

Not far from here, just head north...

Shakespeare woz here

VACANCIES

HOTEL

NORTH

ROMEO VILLE

Some Other Wacky Illinois Town Names:

Assumption
Big Neck
Cereal
Chili
Coffee
Embarrass
Equality
Goofy Ridge

Joy
Love
Normal
Oblong
Peculiar
Roaches
Romeoville

Coffee got its name when a boat filled with coffee traveling up the Wabash River stopped in the area for the night. By morning, the boat had capsized – its coffee dumped into what is now called Coffee Creek!

I'm sure the residents of **Normal** *are* normal, but that's not how the community got its name. A *normal* is a school for training teachers, and this town had one.

Romeoville was originally named Romeo, because of the nearby town of Juliet! But when Juliet later changed its name to Joliet (for explorer Louis Joliet), Romeo changed *its* name to Romeoville! So there!

Illinois

Midwestern State
21st State, Statehood 1818

Info to Know

Disco is located in Hancock County, which was named in honor of John Hancock, one of our nation's founding fathers and the first to sign the Declaration of Independence. His signature was so big and fancy that today people often call a signature a "John Hancock." There is a Hancock County in other states too, like Georgia, Ohio, and Tennessee.

Lay of the Land

Chicago, a city located in northeastern Illinois along the shore of Lake Michigan, is known for its architecture. When the Great Chicago Fire destroyed much of Chicago in 1871, many young, talented architects helped to rebuild it, with some of them becoming the leading architects of the era. Among them was Louis Sullivan, often called the "father of the skyscraper" or the "father of modern architecture." Aside from beautiful buildings, Chicago has parks, sculptures, museums, and lots to do at Navy Pier, which is a 3,000-foot-long pier on the shoreline of Lake Michigan.

Road Trip

Illinois honored John Hancock in yet another way – by naming a skyscraper after him! Chicago's John Hancock Center is 100 stories high, has a really cool architectural design, and the fastest elevator in North America! Ride it 1,000 feet to the John Hancock Observatory, and you'll get spectacular views of the Loop, Chicago's downtown area, and Lake Michigan.

SANTA CLAUS, INDIANA

Santa Claus really did come to town – to one in southern Indiana! It was originally called Santa Fe, but in the mid-1800s, when its residents applied for a post office, they were informed that there already was a Santa Fe, Indiana, and that they'd have to come up with a new town name. They decided to keep the *Santa* part and add *Claus*! Others claim it was Christmas Eve, and the town's residents had gathered to decide once and for all on a name for their community. During their meeting, either sleigh bells rang in the distance and a gust of wind blew the door open, or Santa Claus himself strode into the room. A child shouted, "Santa Claus!" and everyone agreed!

happy snow

POST OFFICE

SANTA CLAUS INDIANA

ELVES ENTRANCE

smell office

In Santa Claus, it's holiday season all year round!

I think Santa Claus, Indiana, should team up with Ho-Ho-Kus, New Jersey, and Jolly, Texas!

the smoke from chimneys in the small town of Aroma

Some Other Wacky Indiana Town Names:

Aroma
Artic
Chili
Correct
Daylight
Economy
Fickle
Gnaw Bone

Pimento
Popcorn
Solitude
Speedway
Surprise
Toad Hop
Toto

Correct was actually incorrect! When applying for a town name in the 1800s, the postmaster of nearby Versailles chose Comet, after Halley's Comet. But his handwriting was a bit messy, and postal officials read it as **Correct**.

When it comes to **Gnaw Bone**, Indiana, no one seems to agree on the origin of its name. Here are three possible explanations: A visitor stopped in the town's sawmill, and was greeted by the owner, who was gnawing on a bone. When the visitor returned later that day, the owner was, once again, gnawing on a bone. The visitor jokingly suggested the town be called Gnaw Bone. The name stuck; The original residents were so poor and hungry, they had to gnaw on bones; The town was actually named Narbonne, after a city in France. But when settlers moved to the area, they incorrectly pronounced it Gnaw Bone.

Speedway is home to the Indianapolis Motor Speedway, where the Indy 500 is held.

IGNORE BONE

GNAW BONE

Indiana

Midwestern State
19th State, Statehood 1816

Info to Know

The Indianapolis 500, or Indy 500, is an automobile race held each Memorial Day weekend in Indianapolis, Indiana. It draws more spectators than any other single sporting event in the U.S.

Lay of the Land

Indiana is famous for its incredible sand dunes. Visit the Indiana Dunes National Lakeshore, in northwest Indiana, where you'll discover dunes almost 200 feet high and have a blast climbing up the dunes and running or rolling down!

Road Trip

The post office in Santa Claus, Indiana, is the only post office in the world with the Santa Claus name. Each year, it receives thousands of letters to Santa from kids across the nation. And Santa even writes back! Cards and letters mailed from the town get stamped with a special Santa Claus postmark, designed by a local high school student as part of an annual competition. To receive this one-of-a-kind postmark, you can bring or mail a letter to the Santa Claus post office. Santa Claus is filled with holiday spirit! As you walk through the town, you'll notice street names with holiday themes, a giant Santa Claus statue, Holiday World & Splashin' Safari theme park, the Santa Claus Museum, and Santa's Candy Castle!

WHAT CHEER, IOWA

Sorry, cheerleaders! This town was not named for you! **What Cheer** (pronounced WAH-cheer) comes from the old English greeting *Wot cher*, meaning "How are you?" or "I hope you're in good cheer!" It seems this greeting was used by the English, Welsh and Scottish miners who came to this town in the late 1800s after a coal mine was discovered in the area. Some suggest Joseph Andrews, a local politician, gave the town its name because of a story connected to his hometown of Providence, Rhode Island. As the story goes, when Roger Williams, Providence's founder, arrived at the place that would become Providence, he was greeted by Narragansett Indians, who welcomed him with "What Cheer, *Netop*!" (*Netop* meant "friend.") The Narragansett had learned the greeting from English settlers.

Some Other Wacky Iowa Town Names:

Coin
Confidence
Correctionville
Cylinder
Diagonal
Gravity

Manly
Nodaway
Rake
Rembrandt
Sergeant Bluff
Story City

Coin got its name after a railroad surveyor found a silver coin while digging in the area, and town residents hoped it would bring them luck. Well, maybe it did! The town received a railroad, which helped it to prosper.

In the 1850s, the town of **Confidence** got its name because residents were confident they would soon have a railroad and that it would bring them prosperity. Unfortunately, they never did get that railroad.

Since residents considered their village to be the center of trade in Washington Township – one that pulled in people from around the area – they named it **Gravity**!

Not only is there a Gravity, Iowa, but there's also a **Newton**, Iowa! (Sir Isaac Newton was the scientist who figured out how gravity works.)

"Snake Alley – a twisting, winding brick street, built in 1894 and known as the "Crookedest Street in the world." I'm feeling dizzy! WOTCHA→

What do you have to say about What Cheer?

Hip, hip, hooray!

Iowa

Midwestern State
29th State, Statehood 1846

Info to Know

On southeast Iowa's bluffs is the city of Burlington, which is home to Snake Alley, a twisting, winding brick street, built in 1894, once recognized by *Ripley's Believe It or Not* as the "Crookedest Street in the World."

Lay of the Land

What Cheer is located in Keokuk County, in southeast Iowa. In southeast Iowa, scenic limestone bluffs – steep riverbanks or cliffs – rise along the Mississippi River.

Road Trip

In Iowa's northeast (also along Mississippi River bluffs) is Effigy Mounds National Monument. Here you'll find prehistoric burial and ceremonial mounds, built by Eastern Woodland American Indians. Many of these mounds, made of earth and stone, are shaped like animals, including birds and bears! Another place to visit in eastern Iowa is Dyersville, famous for its baseball diamond carved out of a cornfield and filmed in the movie *Field of Dreams*.

HOME, KANSAS

Residents had planned on naming their community Dexter, in honor of citizen Thomas Dexter, but as it turned out, the name was already taken. So a meeting was held, and names honoring other prominent citizens were suggested, only to be rejected by the honorees. Finally, residents decided to just name their town after the post office, which was known as the home post office station since it was located in the home of the town's first postmaster, Gottleib Messel. And that's how the residents came to call their community **Home**!

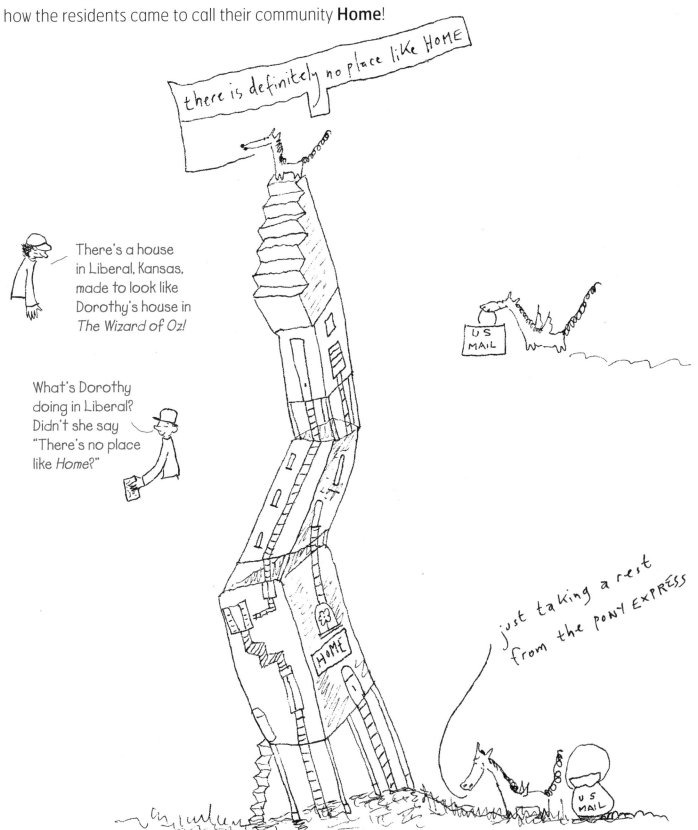

there is definitely no place like HOME

There's a house in Liberal, Kansas, made to look like Dorothy's house in *The Wizard of Oz!*

What's Dorothy doing in Liberal? Didn't she say "There's no place like *Home?*"

just taking a rest from the PONY EXPRESS

US MAIL

HOME

Some Other Wacky Kansas Town Names:

Admire
Bazaar
Big Bow
Bird City
Buttermilk
Coats
Coffeeville

Flush
Good Intent
Liberal
Neutral
Seventy-six
Tennis

Buttermilk was named for local blacksmith, Quincy "Buttermilk" Winningham, who drank lots of buttermilk.

A community in northeast Kansas was supposed to be named for settler Michael Floersch, but by the time postal officials were through with the name it had become **Flush**.

Tennis has nothing to do with the sport. It was named for a manager of the Santa Fe Railway, B.M. Tennis.

POSTCARD
INSIDE
POUCH

Kansas

Midwestern State
34th State, Statehood 1861

Info to Know

The Pony Express was a mail service set up in 1860, which delivered mail by horseback between the eastern United States and the newly settled West. Mail was guaranteed to arrive in ten days — record time in 1860! The delivery was like a relay race. A pony rider, starting in Missouri, would gallop at top speed to a station about 10 to 15 miles away, carrying a pouch of mail. There, he hopped onto a new horse and raced another 10 to15 miles. He continued in this way until he reached his home station, where another rider would take over. The relay continued day and night until the mail reached California. And the same relay was going on in the opposite direction, from California back to Missouri!

Lay of the Land

From Home, travel west on Route 36, also known as the Pony Express Highway because it follows the route of the Pony Express. After about 7 miles you'll reach the city of Marysville, which, in 1860, housed the first home station on the Pony Express route going west. Marysville's home station building still stands and is now a museum.

Road Trip

When you're finished visiting northeast Kansas, move on to central Kansas. Take a trip to Rock City Park, a field of giant globe-shaped rocks, called concretions, in north central Kansas. Then travel south to the Maxwell Wildlife Refuge in central Kansas, to take a tram ride across a prairie and get up close and personal with bison and elk!

Searching for the origin of **Monkey's Eyebrow** can drive you bananas! No one can agree on what it is. Here's one reason given, and if you look on the map, you'll see why: The Ohio River outlines the western end of Kentucky, making it look like the profile of a monkey's face. And the community of Monkey's Eyebrow, in Ballard County, is just where the monkey's eyebrow would be – if monkeys had eyebrows! A similar explanation is that in the late 1800s, people settled in Ballard County on a crescent-shaped hill called Beeler Hill. Tall grass was growing on the hill, and to the settlers, the tall grassy ridge looked like a monkey's eyebrow!

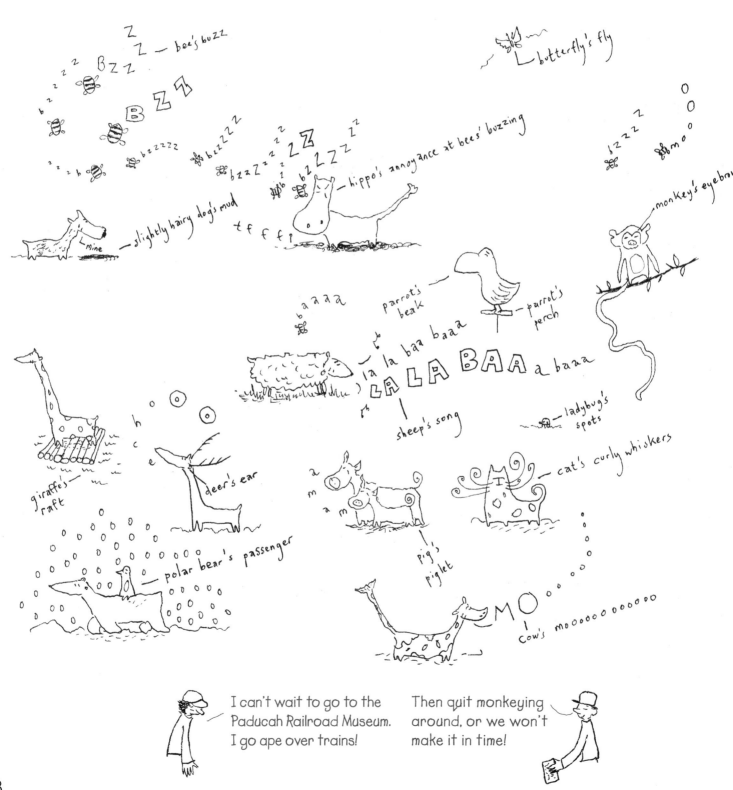

I can't wait to go to the Paducah Railroad Museum. I go ape over trains!

Then quit monkeying around, or we won't make it in time!

Kentucky

Southeastern State
15th State, Statehood 1792

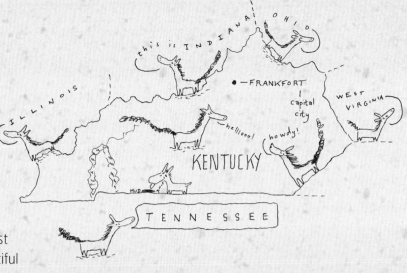

Info to Know

Monkey's Eyebrow is located in Paducah, Kentucky. Paducah, known as Quilt City, U.S.A., is home to the Museum of the American Quilter's Society. It also houses a railroad museum and the River Heritage Museum. Paducah's flood wall, built to protect against flooding from the Ohio River, is decorated with beautiful murals spanning several blocks.

Lay of the Land

Paducah was settled around the year 1815, by American Indian and white settlers. The two groups got along very well and traded goods and services. Paducah was especially attractive to settlers because it was situated where the Ohio and Tennessee rivers meet — a location important for trade.

Road Trip

Louisville, Kentucky, is home to America's most famous horse race, the Kentucky Derby, which takes place annually, on the first Saturday in May. It is often called "The Fastest Two Minutes in Sports," because even though Kentuckians celebrate for two weeks during the Kentucky Derby Festival, the race itself lasts only about two minutes!

Some Other Wacky Kentucky Town Names:

Big Bone
Crummies
Do Stop
Goodluck
Hot Spot
Mudlick
Mummie
Needmore
Oddville
Ordinary
Quicksand
Rowdy
Shoulderblade
Stopover
Typo

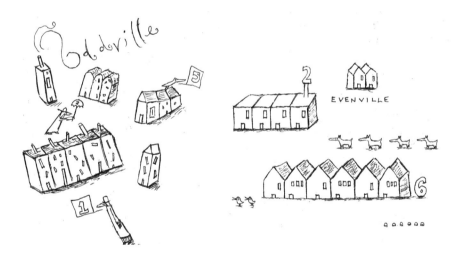

Big Bone, near the Ohio River, was named for the large concentration of bones of prehistoric mammals that were found there.

Residents chose to call their town **Mummie** because of a mummified body early settlers discovered there.

Some say **Ordinary** got its name because it was just an everyday, ordinary place. Others think it was named for a local tavern; in the 1800s, a tavern was called an "ordinary."

Calling all animal lovers! There are Kentucky towns called **Pig**, **Hippo**, **Ibex**, **Butterfly**, and **Parrot**! And for you aspiring artists, there's an **Artville** and a **Paintsville**!

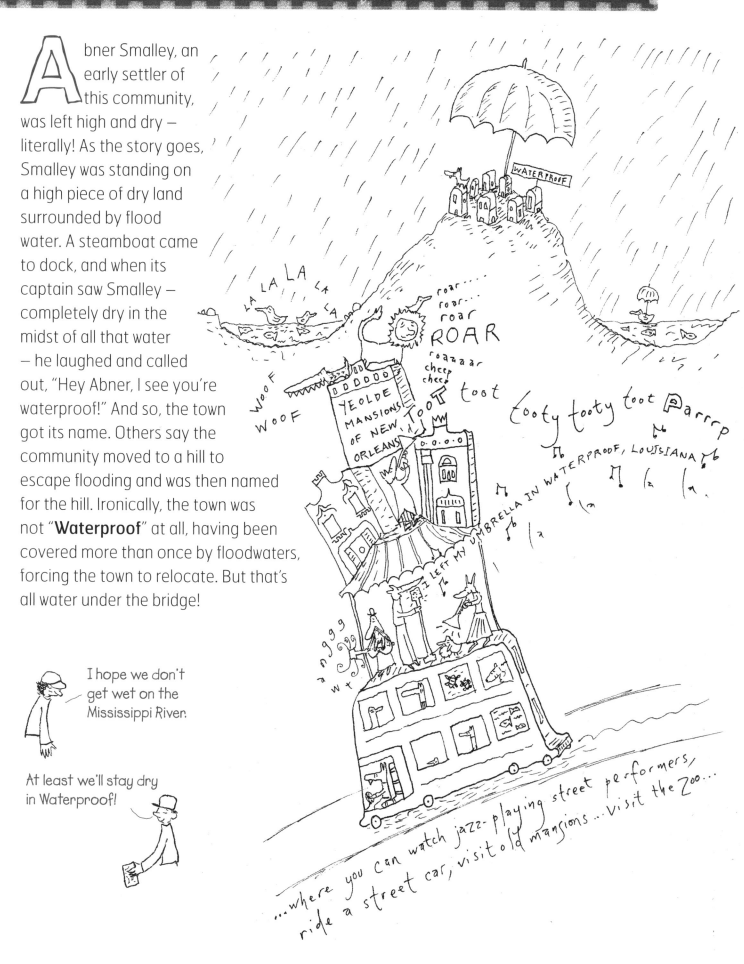

Abner Smalley, an early settler of this community, was left high and dry — literally! As the story goes, Smalley was standing on a high piece of dry land surrounded by flood water. A steamboat came to dock, and when its captain saw Smalley — completely dry in the midst of all that water — he laughed and called out, "Hey Abner, I see you're waterproof!" And so, the town got its name. Others say the community moved to a hill to escape flooding and was then named for the hill. Ironically, the town was not "**Waterproof**" at all, having been covered more than once by floodwaters, forcing the town to relocate. But that's all water under the bridge!

I hope we don't get wet on the Mississippi River.

At least we'll stay dry in Waterproof!

...where you can watch jazz-playing street performers, ride a street car, visit old mansions...visit the zoo...

Some Other Wacky Louisiana Town Names:

Ajax	Many
Bullion	Mix
Cranky Corner	Start
Cut Off	Uncle Sam
Frogmore	Uneedus
Happy Jack	Westwego
Iota	White Castle

Upon receiving a post office and local store, residents (some say the postmaster's daughter) figured their community in northeastern Louisiana was making a fresh start, so they named it **Start**.

Uneedus was named for the slogan of its developers, the Lake Superior Piling Company, which was "You Need Us!"

As some tell it, **Westwego** was a major crossing point for people heading west in the 1800s and was named for the shouts of travelers and/or train conductors yelling, "West we go!"

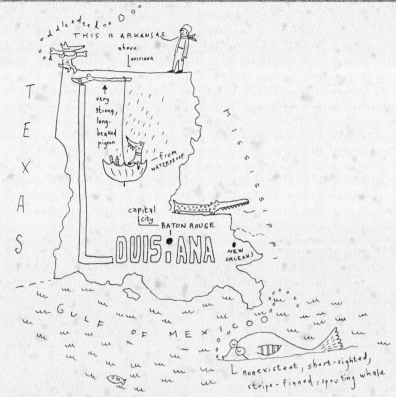

Louisiana

Southeastern State
18th State, Statehood 1812

Info to Know

Waterproof is in eastern Louisiana, on the Mississippi River. There you can take a riverboat ride up and down the mighty Mississippi! Louisiana is known as the birthplace of jazz music. In the early 1900s, African American musicians in New Orleans, Louisiana, began combining different types of music, such as blues, ragtime, and African folk music to create a new kind of music called "jazz." Louis Armstrong, one of the greatest American jazz musicians of all time, was born in New Orleans in 1901.

Lay of the Land

Louisiana is famous for its bayous. A bayou is a slow-moving, swampy body of water. It's usually the offshoot of a river or lake and is found in lowland areas. Bayous are common in states located on the Gulf of Mexico, including Alabama, Florida, Louisiana, Mississippi, and Texas. Take a boat tour of one of the state's many bayous, and you're sure to see — and maybe even feed — some real-live alligators!

Road Trip

New Orleans, in southeastern Louisiana, is an exciting city! There you can watch jazz-playing street performers, ride a street car, view old mansions, wander around the French Quarter's lively streets and alleys, and visit the Audubon Zoo and the Audubon Insectarium, a museum of bugs! New Orleans is especially known for Mardi Gras, a huge festival that takes place every year in February, and includes music, costumes, and parades.

According to legend, **Witch Island** (also called Davis Island) was named in the late 1800s for the woman who purchased the land as her summer home – Mrs. Grace Courtland, also known as the "Witch of Wall Street." Courtland received her nickname because she had an uncanny ability to predict how Wall Street stocks would do. Because of her magic touch with stocks, she had a successful career giving people financial advice. The foundation of Courtland's home still stands today. Some say a strange glow can be seen at times, floating around the area. They say it's Grace Courtland's ghost haunting the island!

the lighthouse featured on the Maine State quarter

Some Other Wacky Maine Town Names:

Bald Head	Owls Head
Bingo	Razorville
Cornville	Robinhood
Dog Town	Slab City
Ducktrap	Strong
Grindstone	Suckerville
Kokadjo	Wonderland
Moosehorn	

Don't confuse **Dog Town**, in Washington County, with Dogtown in Somerset County! Some explain that Dog Town was named for the many dogs in the area, while Dogtown was named for the numerous dogs attracted to the skins and hides of a local tannery.

Kokadjo is actually an abbreviation for Kokadjeweemgwasebemsis! One of the longest place names in the United States, it means "kettle-mountain pond" in the Abenaki Indian language. It was so named because of a kettle-shaped pond or lake in the area.

The many suckerfish in nearby waters gave **Suckerville** its name.

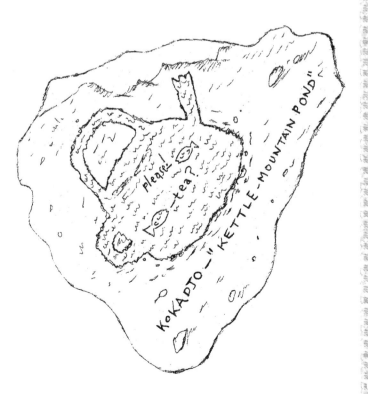

Maine

Northeastern State
23rd State, Statehood 1820

Info to Know

Maine is known for its many lighthouses along its rocky coasts. If you travel about 10 miles north of Witch Island you'll come to Bristol, Maine, where you can visit the beautiful Pemaquid Point Lighthouse. This is the lighthouse featured on the Maine state quarter.

Lay of the Land

The state of Maine is larger than the other five New England states — New Hampshire, Vermont, Massachusetts, Rhode Island, and Connecticut — combined. Almost 90 percent of Maine is forest, much of it pine forests, which is why it's called "The Pine Tree State." Visit the forests of Maine, and you may spot some moose! You can even take a moose tour! (The moose is the state animal.) Many of Maine's residents live along its coasts, where one can go whale and puffin watching! The coastline is 3,500 miles long — that's longer than California's coastline.

Road Trip

There is no end to the hiking you can do in Maine! One of Maine's most popular hiking destinations is Acadia National Park, which lies along the coast, where the mountains rise from the sea! After you've finished hiking, you can learn about lobstering, ride a sailboat called a sloop, rock climb, go sea kayaking, pick blueberries, ride a horse-drawn carriage, and watch a lumberjack show — and that's just for starters! Also in Acadia National Park is Cadillac Mountain, the very first place you can view the sunrise in the United States from October 7th through March 6th!

No, this town was not named for a girdle-wearing tree or even a girdle-growing tree. The reason behind its name is a lot less weird! To girdle a tree means to remove a ring of bark around its trunk in order to kill it, and it seems a tree was once girdled in this area. But who did it and why? No one knows for sure, and there are many different theories. One is that Charles and Mary Bishop girdled a tree to make room for a house they were building. They named their home and property Girdletree Hill. So when a community began to take *shape*, it became known as **Girdletree**. Go figure!

With so much to do in Maryland, will we ever get to Girdletree?

We'll make sure to squeeze it in!

Some Other Wacky Maryland Town Names:

Accident	Friendship
Bestpitch	Halfway
Boring	Parole
Champ	Prettyboy
Chewsville	Secretary
Detour	

Bestpitch has nothing to do with baseball. This hamlet, now deserted, was named for the Bestpitch family.

When Frank Beauchamp applied for a post office, he requested it be named for him. Well, he got his wish – almost. Postal officials thought Beauchamp was too long, so they shortened it to **Champ**.

Secretary was named for the early secretary of the state of Maryland, Lord Henry Sewell.

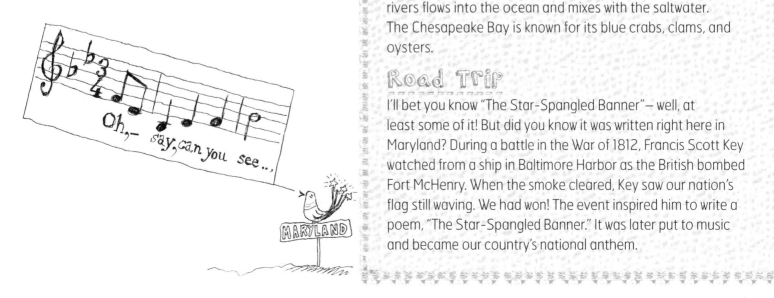

Oh,– say, can you see...,

MARYLAND

nonexsistent, six star-tailed whale

Maryland

Northeastern State
7th State, Statehood 1788

Info to Know

The Mason-Dixon Line – the boundary between Maryland and Pennsylvania – was created by Charles Mason and Jeremiah Dixon, two land surveyors in the 1700s, to settle a land dispute between the colonies of Pennsylvania and Maryland. It also became known as the boundary between the North and the South. And before the Civil War, it was considered to be the division between free and slave states. (Although Maryland is south of the Mason-Dixon line, there is disagreement today about whether or not it is considered a Southern state.)

Lay of the Land

Girdletree is located in Maryand's Lower Eastern Shore, between the Atlantic Ocean and the Chesapeake Bay. The Chesapeake Bay is the largest estuary in the United States. An estuary is a body of water formed when freshwater from rivers flows into the ocean and mixes with the saltwater. The Chesapeake Bay is known for its blue crabs, clams, and oysters.

Road Trip

I'll bet you know "The Star-Spangled Banner"– well, at least some of it! But did you know it was written right here in Maryland? During a battle in the War of 1812, Francis Scott Key watched from a ship in Baltimore Harbor as the British bombed Fort McHenry. When the smoke cleared, Key saw our nation's flag still waving. We had won! The event inspired him to write a poem, "The Star-Spangled Banner." It was later put to music and became our country's national anthem.

Two reasons are given for **Loudville**'s name. One is that Clear Falls, the waterfalls in the area that helped power the town's mills, were very noisy – so loud, in fact, that they kept people up at night! Others say the community was named for Caleb Loud, a man who built and operated various mills in the area, including a button mill, a sawmill, a cotton mill and a paper mill. Residents must have thought his contributions were really something to shout about!

READING, MASSACHUSETTS

Some Other Wacky Massachusetts Town Names:

Barnstable
Blissville
Buzzards Bay
Cow Yard
Fireworks
Gardner
Knightville
Little Neck

Lobsterville
Marblehead
Onset
Orange
Podunk
Reading
Sandwich
Tree of Knowledge Corner

Some explain that **Buzzards Bay** got its name when, in the 1600s, an English explorer (or perhaps colonists) saw seagulls (or perhaps ospreys) flying overhead and thought they were buzzards.

Settlers called their community **Marblehead** because they mistakenly thought the gray granite rocks they saw were marble.

Tree of Knowledge Corner got its name because it was the spot on which an ancient oak tree was located, and people posted messages and letters on or by the tree for residents of Duxbury (where Tree of Knowledge Corner is located).

making a model of THE MAYFLOWER

The people of Loudville might want to spend some time in Quietus, Montana.

I hear you loud and clear!

Massachusetts

Northeastern State
6th State, Statehood 1788

Info to Know

About 12 miles east of Loudville is the Norwottuck Rail Trail. Originally part of the Boston and Maine Railroad, it was paved over and turned into an 11-mile path for hikers, bikers, skaters, cross-country skiers and walkers to enjoy the natural beauty of the area.

Lay of the Land

Boston is the largest city in New England and one of the oldest cities in the country. It lies on the East Coast of the United States, also known as the Eastern Seaboard or Atlantic Seaboard. Major historic events of the American Revolution took place in Boston, like the Boston Tea Party. You can learn about Boston's early history first-hand by walking the Freedom Trail, a path running through downtown Boston and leading to 16 historic sites, like Faneuil Hall (a marketplace and meeting place) and Paul Revere's House.

Road Trip

In 1620, the Mayflower landed on what is now Cape Cod, in the southeast region of Massachusetts. But the Pilgrims settled across the bay, in what became known as Plymouth. Today in Plymouth you can visit Plimoth Plantation, a living history museum, where you'll experience what life was like for the Pilgrims in the New World. At Plimoth Plantation, interpreters dress, speak, and act like the Pilgrims did. You'll feel like you're back in the 1600s. You can even climb aboard a replica of the Mayflower!

BRAVO, MICHIGAN

Although this community may deserve applause, its name has nothing to do with cheering crowds. It was named for those brave pioneers who cleared the trees and built a community in the wilderness, because while *bravo* is a shout of approval, it is also an Italian word that literally means "brave" or "bold." **Bravo** was originally called Sherman, either after a resident, or after William T. Sherman, a Union general in the Civil War. But when residents applied for a post office, they were told there already was a Sherman, Michigan. So Bravo it became. Bravo!

Bravo for Bravo and the whole state of Michigan!

What cheer! Oops—that's in Iowa.

Air Zoo
BRAVO, MICHIGAN

MICHIGAN

up up and a wayyy

Some Other Wacky Michigan Town Names:

Aloha
Bad Axe
Bliss
Brethren
Butternut
Dice
Echo
Grape

Hatmaker
Kalamazoo
Maybee
Payment
Pigeon
Waltz
Wooden Shoe Village

Because of all the hills, your voice can really echo in **Echo**!

Grape got its name because it's located in Raisinville Township!

Wooden Shoe Village was named for Wooden Shoe, a brand of beer made in nearby Ohio, which was popular among loggers working in the area.

Michigan

Midwestern State
26th State, Statehood 1837

Info to Know

Bravo is located in Allegan County, in the southwestern region of Michigan's Lower Peninsula. Also in this region is Battle Creek — nicknamed Cereal City because it's home to Kellogg's and Post cereals — and Kalamazoo, which has many interesting museums, like the Air Zoo, with its historical and rare aircraft, flight simulators, and indoor amusement park rides, and the Gilmore Car Museum, rated one of the 10 best large automobile museums in the country!

Lay of the Land

Michigan is the only state split into two parts, the Upper Peninsula and Lower Peninsula. A peninsula is a body of land surrounded by water on three sides. The two peninsulas are connected by the Mackinac Bridge. Once a year, on Labor Day, 50,000 to 65,000 people participate in the Mackinac Bridge Walk, where they walk the length of the bridge, about 5 miles. Another way to get from one peninsula to the other is by ferry.

Road Trip

Michigan is called the Great Lakes State because it borders four of the five Great Lakes: Erie, Huron, Michigan and Superior. These lakes were a major travel route for ships in the late 1800s and early 1900s, and therefore, also the site of shipwrecks, many of which have been preserved by the lakes' extremely cold waters. Divers come from all around the country to explore them. You can explore the shipwrecks too, by taking a two-hour glass-bottom boat tour in the Alger Underwater Preserve in Munising, Michigan!

No reason to lose sleep over how this city got its name! **Sleepy Eye** was named in honor of Chief Sleepy Eye, or *Ish-Tak-Ha-Ba*, a Dakota chief who received his name because of his droopy eyelids. Chief Sleepy Eye was a very peaceful man and a good friend to the white settlers. A local lake was also named for him. Others say the lake was named for Chief Sleepy Eye, and the town was named after the lake. Apparently, not everyone sees eye to eye!

and I sit sleepy-eyed in my fine nest...

and sleepily watch clouds...

and smoke from chimneys...

and cars and people coming and going...

START

I am a sleepy-eyed bird

The residents of Sleepy Eye should go to Good Night, Colorado!

And in the morning they should head out to Wide Awake!

then I sleepy-eyed, sleepily sleep

END

PS: sometimes I fly too

Minnesota

Midwestern State
32nd State, Statehood 1858

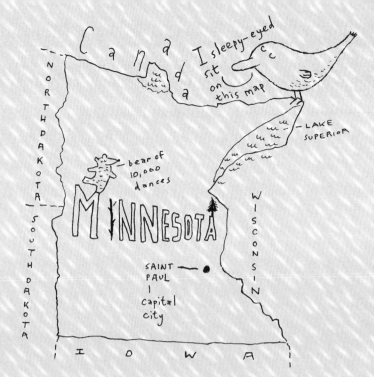

Info to Know

In Sleepy Eye, you'll find two interesting statues. One is a bronze statue of Chief Sleepy Eye. The other is a colorful statue of the famous *Peanuts* cartoon character, Linus! The Linus statue honors cartoonist Linus Maurer, who was born and raised in Sleepy Eye. Charles Schulz, the creator of *Peanuts*, taught cartooning with Linus Maurer and was a good friend of his. They were such good friends, in fact, that Schulz named the Linus character after him!

Lay of the Land

Minnesota is known for its many lakes. In fact, it's nicknamed the "Land of 10,000 Lakes," although it really has closer to 15,000 lakes! Minnesota is also the starting point for three great rivers: the Red River of the North, the St. Lawrence, and the mighty Mississippi River.

Road Trip

If you like the Linus statue in Sleepy Eye, you can see bronze statues of all the *Peanuts* characters in Saint Paul, Minnesota, where Charles Schulz was born. Saint Paul is Minnesota's capital city, while nearby Minneapolis is the state's largest city. Together, Saint Paul and Minneapolis are known as the Twin Cities. In Saint Paul during the winter, you can take part in the Saint Paul Winter Carnival which includes a huge treasure hunt, sleigh rally, ice palace and an incredible ice sculpting competition! In summer, don't miss the Minnesota State Fair, also known as the "Great Minnesota Get-Together." It's a twelve-day fair with a wide range of exhibits and activities. You might want to check out the butter sculptures or the deep-fried candy bars!

Some Other Wacky Minnesota Town Names:

Artichoke	Moonshine
Assumption	Outing
Ball Club	Rollingstone
Blackberry	Split Hand
Downer	Staples
Excel	Tenstrike
Great Scott	Twig

The board of county commissioners was in charge of naming a township. A favorite expression of one of the board members was "**Great Scott**!" So the board decided that that would be the name!

No rockstars here! **Rollingstone** was named for the river *Eyan-omen-man-met-pah,* meaning "the stream where the stone rolls" in the Dakota Indian language.

There are different reasons given for the naming of **Tenstrike**. According to one, in the late 1800s a pioneer, bowled over by the area's beauty, told fellow pioneers that they'd sure made a great move, or a ten-strike, by settling there. According to another, it was simply named for the strike one gets in bowling.

HOT COFFEE, MISSISSIPPI

The story behind **Hot Coffee** might just perk you up! In the 1800s, this area of land stood on a major commercial route. Farmers traveled through it on their way to Ellisville, a town and marketplace where farmers sold and traded crops. One day, a man many believe was named Levi Davis decided to open a store (some say inn) at a spot on the road to Ellisville, so travelers could take a break from their long journey and enjoy a nice hot cup of coffee. The farmers looked forward to this stop and would reassure each other that it was "just a few more miles to the hot coffee." Soon, the stop became known as Hot Coffee, and the name spilled over to the town that grew up around it!

Zzzzzzz

Hey! Wake up, and smell Hot Coffee!

Some Other Wacky Mississippi Town Names:

Alligator	Onward
Arm	Progress
Birdie	Shivers
Dont	Soso
Ecru	Veto
Eggville	Whynot
Hard Cash	Zero
Midnight	

According to legend, as citizens sat around thinking of a name for their town, one person would make a suggestion, and another would say, "*Don't* name it that." This went on and on, until residents agreed to just call their town **Dont**!

As the story goes, when a post office was opened in an area in Franklin County, residents suggested many names, but all were vetoed. So postal officials decided to name it **Veto**!

Soso was so named because when people would ask one of the early residents how he was feeling, he would always answer, "so-so."

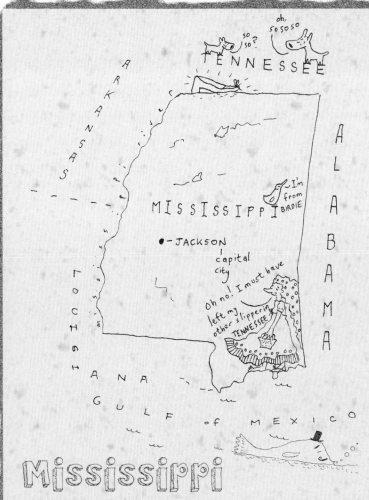

Mississippi
Southeastern State
20th State, Statehood 1817

Info to Know
About a two-hour drive from Hot Coffee is Jackson, Mississippi's capital and most populated city. Jackson has many museums, historic areas — including Civil War and Civil Rights sites — a hundred-acre zoo, and lots of places to hear great music, including jazz, gospel, and blues.

Lay of the Land
The Mississippi Delta is an area of land in northwestern Mississippi, between the Yazoo and Mississippi Rivers. The land of the Mississippi Delta is very flat and its soil extremely fertile — great for growing things. That's why it was home to the large wheat and cotton plantations.

Road Trip
Mississippi, or more specifically, the Mississippi Delta, is considered the birthplace of blues music. The blues evolved from songs sung by African slaves as they labored in the fields of the Southern plantations, and is the foundation of lots of other kinds of music, like jazz, rhythm and blues, rock and roll, and hip hop. To find out more about the blues, you can visit the Delta Blues Museum in Clarksdale, Mississippi, in the heart of the Mississippi Delta.

PECULIAR, MISSOURI

Peculiar was named in the 1800s, after the postmaster's suggestions for a town name kept getting rejected. The frustrated postmaster finally sent a letter to the Post Office Department in Washington, D.C., saying that he didn't care what name they chose, as long as it was peculiar. So **Peculiar** it became! In another version of the story, the postal officials were the ones that suggested coming up with a name that was peculiar, and the townspeople were the ones that took the suggestion literally. Interestingly, Peculiar, Missouri, is not far from Normal, Illinois! And there is a Missouri town named Lewis and another one named Clark!

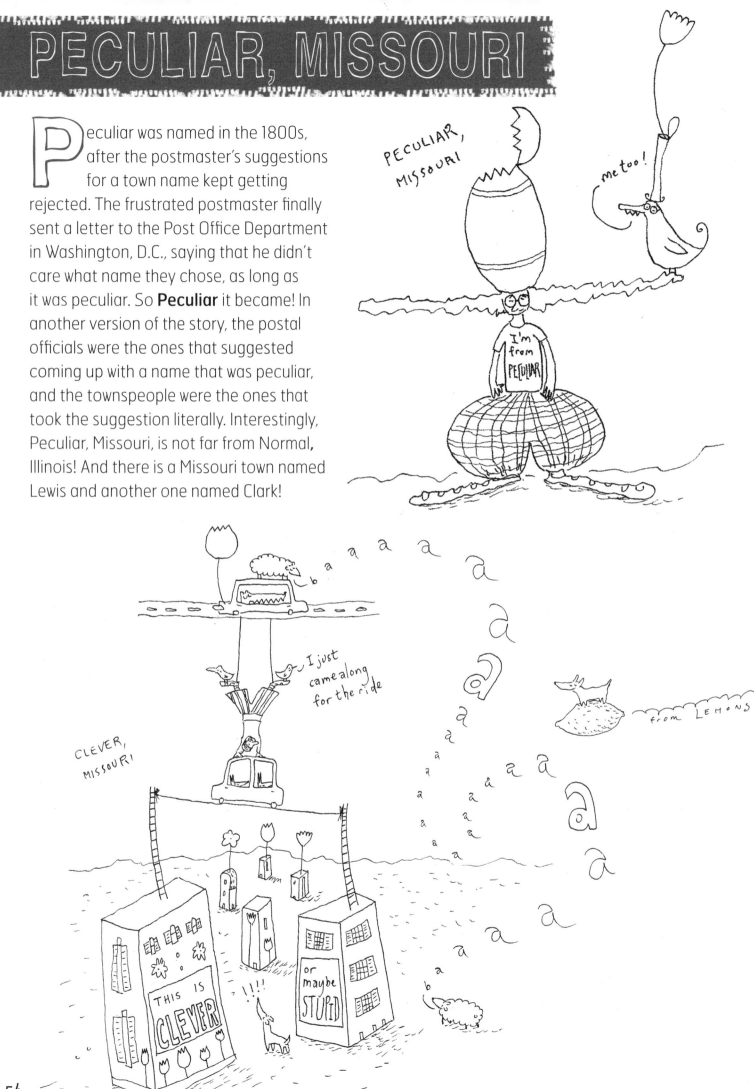

Some Other Wacky Missouri Town Names:

Black Jack
Bland
Boss
Clever
Competition
Cureall
Enough

Frankenstein
Humansville
Lemons
Rescue
Tightwad
Tuxedo

Black Jack is not named after the card game, but after a row of blackjack oak trees that served as a natural landmark for early pioneers.

Cureall was named for the mineral springs in the area, which were believed to have healing powers that would cure all.

Feeling frightened? Getting goose bumps? Have no fear! **Frankenstein**, Missouri, is no haunted hamlet! In fact, it has absolutely nothing to do with monsters. Gottfried Franken, an early German settler, donated land and stone for his neighborhood's first church. In German, the word for stone is *stein*. And that's how Frankenstein was created! (Some say the "stein" was added later because of the area's rocky terrain.)

All this talk about Frankenstein, Missouri, makes me want to hurry on to Mummie, Kentucky!

lemons ahoy!

lemon air ship

LEMONS, MISSOURI

fresh lemonade SOLD HERE!

bitter night hotel

Missouri

Midwestern State
24th State, Statehood 1821

Info to Know

In Mary Shelley's novel, *Frankenstein*, Frankenstein is actually the doctor who creates the monster, not the monster itself.

Lay of the Land

The nation's two largest rivers, the Missouri River and Mississippi River, run through the state of Missouri. The Missouri River, traveled by Lewis and Clark in the early 1800s, runs from southern Montana to St. Louis, Missouri. It then flows into the Mississippi River. The Mississippi River is one of the most important rivers in the U.S. It flows north to south, from Minnesota to New Orleans. On its way down, it travels along the border shared by Missouri and Illinois.

Road Trip

Mark Twain, the famous author of *The Adventures of Tom Sawyer* and *The Adventures of Huckleberry Finn*, among others, lived in Hannibal, Missouri, as a boy, where he had many adventures. If you visit Hannibal, in northern Missouri, you can take a Mark Twain riverboat ride, visit the Mark Twain Boyhood Home and Museum, and explore caves, like Cameron Cave, as Mark Twain did as a boy. Mark Twain's real name was Samuel Clemens.

HUNGRY HORSE, MONTANA

If you're hungry for a dramatic place-name story, listen to this! In the harsh, snowy winter of 1900-1901, Tex and Jerry (some say Terry), two work horses used for hauling logs or equipment in the wilderness area of the Flathead River, wandered off. They were found one month later, thin, weak, disheveled and starved, but to everyone's surprise, alive. With time, good care and food, they were nursed back to health. And so, the town that grew up in the area was named **Hungry Horse**, and so were the nearby creek, lake, and dam. It's true - no horsing around!

Some Other Wacky Montana Town Names:

Big Arm	Pony
Checkerboard	Powderville
Elmo	Pray
Joe	Racetrack
Moccasin	Rocky Boy
Muddy	Two Dot
Plentywood	Zero

TWO DOT, MONTANA

Two dot or not two dot? THAT IS THE QUESTION

AM I ONE OF YOURS?

In 1993, the town of Ismay, Montana, unofficially renamed itself **Joe**, Montana, for former NFL star quarterback, Joe Montana! The town has since gone back to calling itself Ismay.

Cattleman George "Two-Dot" Wilson branded his cows and horses with two dots, which is how **Two Dot** got its name.

When a railroad was first built in the area of **Zero**, there was nothing – zero – for miles around!

BIG ARM, MONTANA

Statue of BIG ARM FLORENCE who (allegedly) pulled two trucks from a snow drift with just one arm

BIG ARM FLORENCE

* not related to SMALL ARM LAWRENCE who rescued two baby birds from a hole in a tree trunk (allegedly)

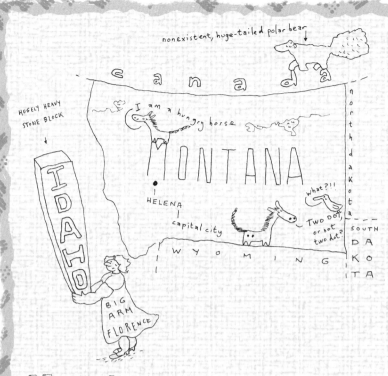

nonexistent, huge-tailed polar bear

HUGELY HEAVY STONE BLOCK

c a n a d a

north dakota

I am a hungry horse

MONTANA

HELENA

capital city

what?!!

Two dot, or not two dot?

SOUTH DAKOTA

WYOMING

IDAHO

BIG ARM FLORENCE

Montana

Western State
41st State, Statehood 1889

Info to Know

You can take a guided tour of the Hungry Horse Dam, the 11th-largest concrete dam in the country, and visit the 34-mile-long Hungry Horse Reservoir. The dam and reservoir are surrounded by mountains offering great fishing and hiking in the area. Hungry Horse is also known for its huckleberry milkshakes! Huckleberries are native to northwestern Montana, growing on mountainsides in and around Glacier National Park. Roadside stands sell every huckleberry food imaginable, including jellies, honey, candy, tea, barbecue sauce, and everyone's favorite – milkshakes!

Lay of the Land

Just 10 miles east of Hungry Horse, in northwestern Montana, is Glacier National Park, one of the most beautiful national parks in the country. Its picturesque landscape includes glaciers, waterfalls, mountains, and meadows. It also has mountain goats and grizzly bears! Visitors can learn about nature, geology, and American Indians as they hike its 700 miles of trails.

Road Trip

Montana is also known for its ghost towns! If you want to see lots of these abandoned boomtown villages, visit Philipsburg, in southwestern Montana. When you're done touring its many ghost towns, head over to Philipsburg's historic downtown area to see restored buildings from the era. And be sure to check out the Montana Ghost Town Hall of Fame!

It should come as no surprise that people can't agree on how this village got its name. Some say it was named by settlers who were pleasantly surprised by the high quality of its land. Others suggest that when early settler George Miller arrived in 1881, he was surprised to find that the area's river had lots of water flowing – enough to power a mill. Still others explain that the village was far from other towns, and as new settlers arrived, they were surprised to see a working mill so far from civilization. The mill came to be known as the Surprise Mill. And the town that developed there was named – not surprisingly – **Surprise!**

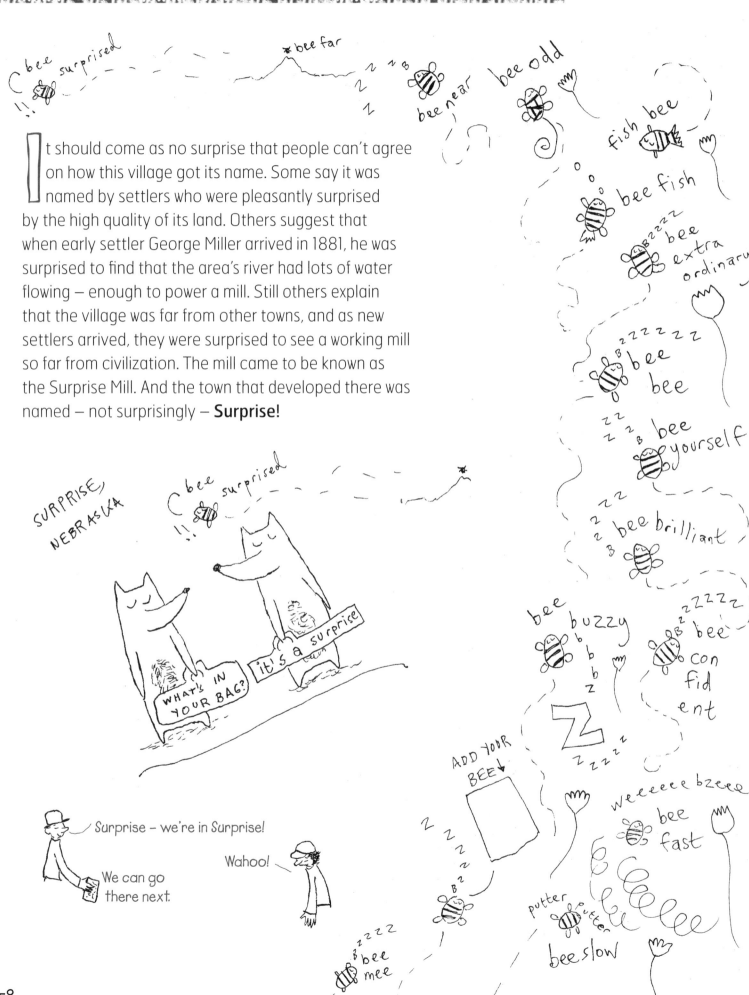

Some Other Wacky Nebraska Town Names:

Bee	Mascot
Champion	Quick
Cook	Roach
Friend	Wahoo
Gross	Worms
Hazard	Wynot
Magnet	

Nothing disgusting here! **Gross** was named for postmaster B.B. Gross.

Magnet was so named to attract settlers!

No one can agree on the origin of the name **Wahoo**. Some reasons given are: It comes from an Indian word meaning "burning bush;" It was a kind of shrub used by local Indians for medicinal purposes; It is derived from an Indian word meaning "fairly level land" (although the area is quite rocky!); It's an Indian word having to do with a certain species of elm.

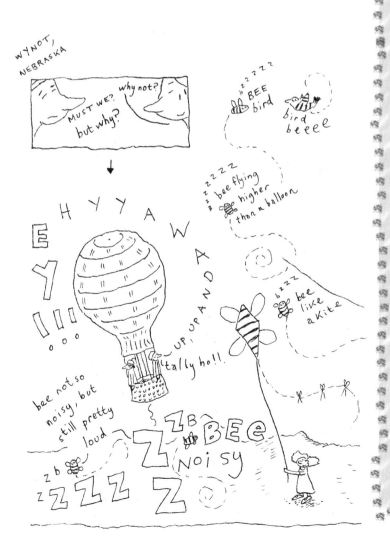

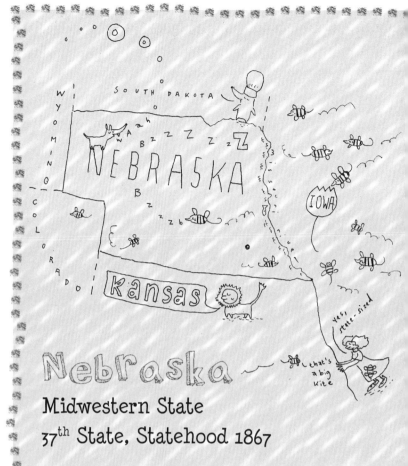

Nebraska

Midwestern State
37th State, Statehood 1867

Info to Know

When settlers first arrived in Nebraska, they saw grassy prairies with few trees. Lacking wood for houses, many built homes from sod, or dirt and grass, which they dug from the prairies, earning them the nickname "Sodbusters!"

Lay of the Land

Chimney Rock, in western Nebraska, is an eye-catching, pillar-like geological formation, made of clay, volcanic ash, and sandstone. Chimney Rock was perhaps the most famous landmark on the Oregon Trail and the California Trail — trails used by settlers in the 1800s journeying to the American West.

Road Trip

Surprise is located in eastern Nebraska. Also in the region is Omaha, Nebraska's largest city, on the shore of the Missouri River. Omaha is home to the famous Henry Doorly Zoo. With its focus on conservation and research, the Henry Doorly Zoo is considered to be one of the best zoos in the country. A highlight is the Lied Jungle, the world's largest indoor rainforest! Visitors use all their senses to experience the natural rainforest habitats of Asia, Africa, and South America!

JACKPOT, NEVADA

If you thought **Jackpot** was named for the slot machine, you're right on the money! Many explain that this isolated town, located on the Nevada–Idaho border, got its name in 1959, when a cabin filled with slot machines was built. It was the only place to gamble in the area and was opened at a time when neighboring Idaho was cracking down on illegal gambling. It soon became a popular place with people, especially Idahoans, looking to win the jackpot! The town was originally called *Unincorporated Town Number 1*!

JACKPOT, NEVADA (the town was originally called Unincorporated Town Number 1)

I want to change my name to: UNINCORPORATED HUMAN NUMBER ONE

JACKPOT, NEVADA

DING -ding -DING

...three!

far away on the other side of town...

HOORAY! Nestor's laid three eggs!

Jackpot has an 18-hole golf course!

I hope you're not bluffing!

DINNER STATION, NEVADA

ALL ABOARD!

welcome to DINNER STATION

Nevada

Western State
36st State, Statehood 1864

Info to Know

Jackpot is part of Cowboy Country, the name given to northern Nevada because its mountain ranges and valleys have been home to cowboys and cowgirls for years. Another town in Cowboy Country is McDermitt, which straddles the Nevada-Oregon border and is filled with a mix of Indian culture and cowboy history. McDermitt's two biggest events are the Indian Rodeo and the Twin States Stampede – Nevada's longest-running rodeo!

Lay of the Land

Jackpot, now a resort town, is located in northeastern Nevada, a very remote region of the state filled with the untouched wilderness of mountains, canyons, grass and wildflowers. The Jarbridge Wilderness, one of the most remote areas in the state and perhaps even the country, is located in this region, in the mountains southwest of Jackpot. The Jarbridge Wilderness is part of the Humboldt-Toiyabe National Forest, the largest national forest in the U.S., outside of Alaska.

Road Trip

Two famous places to visit in southern Nevada are Las Vegas and the Hoover Dam. Las Vegas is the largest city in Nevada.

It's famous for its casino resorts and entertainment. There's lots for kids to do in and outside Las Vegas, like dune buggy riding in the desert and jeep riding through nearby Red Rock Canyon! The Hoover Dam, on the Colorado River, is one of the world's largest dams and an engineering masterpiece! It supplies water and power to Nevada, Arizona, and southern California. The dam created Lake Mead, the largest man-made lake in the United States.

Some Other Wacky Nevada Town Names:

Cal-Nev-Ari
Dinner Station
Duckwater
Lovelock
Pronto
Searchlight

Shanty Town
Stagecoach
Steamboat
Tungsten
Weed Heights

Cal-Nev-Ari stands for California, Nevada, and Arizona, because it's located near the point where these states meet.

There are many theories about how **Searchlight** got its name. According to one theory, it was named after gold miner Floyd Searchlight. Others suggest it was named for a brand of matches. But probably the most agreed-upon story among long-time residents of Searchlight is that the community got its name when a group of unsuccessful miners said there might be gold in the area, but one would need a searchlight to find it! When Fred Colton, founder of Searchlight, found gold ore, he remembered this joke and named the area Searchlight.

The town of **Steamboat** was named for Steamboat Springs, an area with many hot springs, where steam rises up from the water like a steamboat.

STAGECOACH, NEVADA

* SIZES MAY VARY

SANDWICH, NEW HAMPSHIRE

The story behind **Sandwich** is not too hard to swallow! In 1763, Benning Wentworth, the colonial governor of New Hampshire, granted permission for a town to be built on a plot of land in eastern New Hampshire. It was named Sandwich in honor of John Montagu, the Fourth Earl of Sandwich, an Englishman who helped command the British Royal Navy. When the land was surveyed, it was found to be full of mountains and rocks, which would make it difficult to settle. So in 1764, additional land was granted, making Sandwich one of the largest towns in New Hampshire. The first settlers arrived in 1767, and by 1830 it was a thriving community.

SANDWICH - NEW HAMPSHIRE

I don't like the look of that... grumble grump grump

WORLD'S CURLIEST SANDWICH

← WORLD'S SURLIEST MAN WITCH

Visiting Sandwich has gotten me in the mood for a sandwich!

So, let's head over to Rye, New Hampshire, then Mustard, Pennsylvania, and Mayo, Maryland!

And don't forget Turkey, Texas!

weeeeee

WASH HAIR CINEMA
now showing
TOTAL AVOIDANCE

SOAP STORES

MUSEUM of BUBBLES

MUSEUM OF TAP

tippety tappety   tappety tippety   clippety cloppety

HOTEL WASH WELL

BATH, NEW HAMPSHIRE

Some Other Wacky New Hampshire Town Names:

Bath
Breakfast Hill
Cowbell Corners
Happy Corner
Horse Corner
Lost Nation
Rye
Sandwich Landing
Snowville

Cowbell Corners was named for a bell that hung in the town's woolen mill.

Happy Corner earned its name by being a happy place for residents who gathered in a local store, chatting, joking, and playing cards. Others say they gathered in the home of a neighbor to sing and dance. Either way, they were all having a happy time!

A story is told that **Horse Corner** got its name when a Revolutionary War soldier deserted his post and stole a horse in order to ride home to Concord. Some say he eventually abandoned the horse and left it in the *corner* of a cellar hole. Others explain that *corner* was just a common way of saying crossroads.

HAPPY CORNER, NEW HAMPSHIRE

New Hampshire

Northeastern State
9th State, Statehood 1788

Info to Know

The town of Sandwich was not the only thing named after John Montagu, the Fourth Earl of Sandwich. Montagu helped finance English explorer Captain James Cook's explorations, so when Cook discovered the Hawaiian Islands, in 1778, he named them the Sandwich Islands! Guess what else was named for John Montagu — the sandwich! According to legend, while gambling one day, Montagu asked his servant to bring him a slice of meat between two pieces of toasted bread. This was so he could eat with one hand and continue the game with the other and not have to take a lunch break!

Lay of the Land

Sandwich sits on the shore of Squam Lake (the second largest lake in New Hampshire), between the Lakes Region and White Mountains Region. It is surrounded by hills and valleys, hiking trails and beautiful views. Some of the festivities that take place in and around Sandwich are Old Home Week, Sandwich Fair, and the Sandwich Notch Sled Dog Race! Sandwich has been designated as a historic town.

Road Trip

New Hampshire's White Mountains region is popular with tourists throughout the year. An exciting attraction in this region is the Mountain Coaster, a roller coaster built right on Attitash Mountain! Riders board a two-person coaster that pulls them 1,430 feet up the Attitash Mountain on stainless steel rails, providing spectacular views of the White Mountains. Then riders zoom 2,880 feet down the mountain, through curves, over dips, and through the forested mountain terrain!

No need to run from your cheesecake! It's not about to quiver, shake, or split! But the number of explanations given for this town name is enough to make you quake! Some say **Cheesequake** got its name because the area is marshy and has "*quaking* bogs"— strong mats of moss that form on ponds, and shake and quiver when you walk on them! But many disagree and explain that it has American Indian roots. The Lenni-Lenape Indians used to hunt and fish in the area, and some say Cheesequake is derived from *Cheseh-oh-ke*, a Lenni-Lenape word meaning "highland" or "upland." But most explain it's derived from the name of a Lenni-Lenape sub-tribe, the *Chichequaas*. When Dutch and European immigrants came to the area in the 1800s, they named it for the *Chichequaas*, but spelled it *Chesquaacks*. And by the 1900s, it had turned into Cheesequake!

New Jersey

Northeastern State
3rd State, Statehood 1787

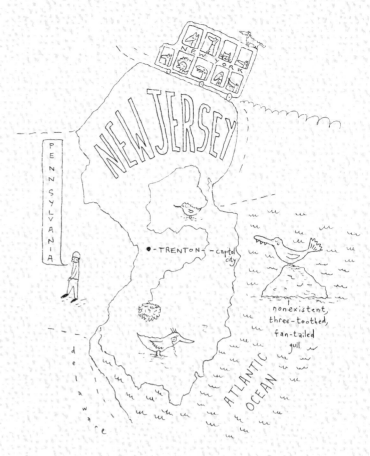

Info to Know

Just northeast of Cheesequake is Cheesequake State Park. It has open fields, rolling hills, marshes, and a hardwood forest. It's also home to red foxes, white-tailed deer, and almost 200 species of birds. Northwest of Cheesequake State Park is the township of Edison, named after Thomas Edison, one of the world's greatest inventors. Edison Township is home to Thomas Edison's famous laboratory in Menlo Park, where Edison worked on hundreds of inventions, earning him the nickname "The Wizard of Menlo Park." His inventions include the first practical electric lighting system, the phonograph, and motion pictures. You can visit Edison Memorial Tower and Museum to learn more about Thomas Edison and his work.

Lay of the Land

In northwestern New Jersey, on the border of New Jersey and Pennsylvania, is the Delaware Water Gap. A water gap is where a river carves through a mountain ridge. In the Delaware Water Gap, the Delaware River cuts through the Kittatinny Mountains, a ridge of the Appalachian Mountains. The Delaware Water Gap is a popular area for outdoor activities, from hiking and rock climbing to canoeing and tubing!

Road Trip

New Jersey's Atlantic Coast, also called the New Jersey Shore, is more than 127 miles long, and filled with beaches, boardwalks, and attractions. Wildwood, a resort city in the Southern Jersey Shore region, has 38 blocks of white sand beaches, a boardwalk almost 2 miles long, carnival games, and amusement park and water park rides! If you visit Atlantic City, further north along the shore, you might feel as if you're walking through a life-sized Monopoly game! That's because the streets in Monopoly, like Boardwalk and Atlantic Avenue, were named after streets in Atlantic City!

Some Other Wacky New Jersey Town Names:

Bargaintown
Bivalve
Brick
Califon
Changewater
Cologne
Double Trouble
Friendship
Good Intent
Ho-Ho-Kus
Scrappy Corner
Timbuctoo
Turpentine

Bargaintown was appropriately named when its plots of land were sold at bargain prices!

As the story goes, **Califon** was originally named *California*, but when a railroad sign announcing the town name was being painted, the painters ran out of room. So they shortened the name to *Califon*!

Good Intent was named for the Good Intent Woolen Factory.

PIE TOWN, NEW MEXICO

There are different versions of the story of how **Pie Town** got its name, but most of them go something like this: In the early 1920s, a man named Clyde Norman moved to the area from Texas. He came looking for gold, but he couldn't find any. Instead, he opened a business. Some say it was a general store. Others say it was a gas station. Either way, when there was a lull in business, Norman would bake and sell pies. Word got out, and people started coming to the area for his pies. As the town grew, it needed a name, and it was clear what that name would be! Pie Town!

PIE TOWN, NEW MEXICO

Cinema GOOD Filling

NOW SHOWING GOODFILLAS

Madame Cherry's DREAM PIE EMPORIUM

THICK CRUST HOTEL

← MADAME CHERRY

WeL COME to PIE TOWN

PIE POST

A FEW ALTERNATIVE PIES...

ONE STAR PIE

— TWO STAR PIE

SNAKES & LADDERS PIE

CHECKERBOARD PIE

PITCH FORK PIE

simply the best
PIE PIE

MUD PIE

cloud pie

— NEW MEXICO PIE

We can't leave yet. I haven't sampled all the pies!

New Mexico

Southwestern State
47th State, Statehood 1912

Info to Know

As time passed, Pie Town's population shrank, and pies were no longer being sold. Lucky for us though, the pies are back in Pie Town! Today you can get them at the Daily Pie Café and the Pie-O-Neer, where you can choose from a large variety of flavors. You may want to try New Mexican apple, peanut butter, banana dream cream, or blueberry and grape! The biggest event in Pie Town is the annual Pie Festival, which takes place in September. Of course, one of the events is a pie-eating contest!

Lay of the Land

Pie Town is located on the Continental Divide. This is an imaginary line running along the crest of the Rocky Mountains, from Canada to New Mexico. Along this line, waters flow in opposite directions. Water falling east of the Continental Divide flows east, into the Atlantic Ocean. Water falling west of the divide flows west, into the Pacific Ocean. The Continental Divide is also called the Great Divide. People hike and bike the Continental Divide, and many stop in Pie Town along the way!

Road Trip

New Mexico is home to 19 American Indian pueblos. *Pueblo* means "village" in Spanish. It was also the name given by Spanish explorers to a group of American Indian tribes. You can visit Taos Pueblo, which has the largest surviving multi-storied Pueblo structure, and the Acoma Pueblo, built on a massive sandstone mesa. Acoma is one of the oldest continuously inhabited communities in the United States.

Some Other Wacky New Mexico Town Names:

Arms
Bent
Brick
Chili
Fruitland
Highway
Hope

House
Lingo
Rodeo
Texico
Top of the World
Truth or Consequences
X Ray

Highway was located along a state highway.

Texico has nothing to do with gas stations. This city was so named because it's located on the Texas-New Mexico border.

Truth or Consequences was named after a popular radio quiz show of the 1940s and 1950s. Originally called Hot Springs, this small city changed its name when the host of *Truth or Consequences* offered free publicity to the town that would name itself after the show. In 1950, Hot Springs took them up on their offer! The show is no longer on, but the town kept the name.

NEVERSINK, NEW YORK

Over the years, **Neversink** has been spelled and pronounced in never-ending ways, including Nevisinck, Naewersink, Narvasing, Narvavasing, Neiversink and Never Sink! There are different explanations as to the name's origin, but all relate to the river that runs through the town—also called Neversink. Some think *Neversink* describes a continually running stream that never sinks into the ground, or a stream that runs so rapidly objects are carried away instead of sinking. But many others believe it comes from an Indian word; perhaps *Ne-wa-sink*, an Algonquian word meaning "Mad River," or *Mahackamack*, as the river was labeled on an early map. Other suggested definitions of the Indian word (whatever word that may be) are "highland between waters," "water between highlands," "fishing place," and "at the point." And that's every explanation but the kitchen sink!

New York

Northeastern State
11th State, Statehood 1788

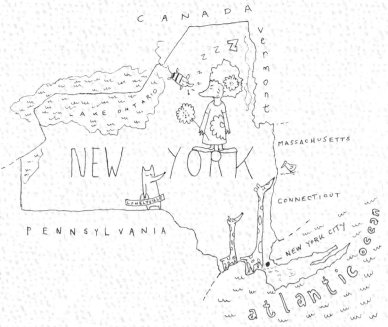

Info to Know

The Neversink River is considered by many to be the birthplace of American fly fishing. Another Neversink claim to fame is its annual Little World's Fair, which has been held for over 130 years. This August fair includes a wide range of activities, including horse shows, goat and sheep shows, juggling shows, a tractor parade, pie auction, rides, and fireworks.

Lay of the Land

Neversink is located in the heart of the Catskill Mountains, a range with stunning peaks, steep-sloped mountains, cliffs, and waterfalls. And if you like waterfalls, travel all the way east to another place of natural beauty, Niagara Falls, on the United States-Canada border. Niagara Falls is made up of three breathtaking waterfalls — the American Falls and Bridal Veil Falls in New York, and the Horseshoe Falls in Ontario, Canada.

Road Trip

Southeast of Neversink is New York City, the largest city in the United States. New York City is divided up into five sections called boroughs: the Bronx, Brooklyn, Queens, Staten Island, and Manhattan. In Brooklyn, you can visit Coney Island, with its amusement park rides, carnival games, beach, and boardwalk. In the late 1800s and early 1900s, it had three amusement parks and hundreds of attractions. Referred to as the "playground of the world," it drew millions of visitors! You can also walk the Brooklyn Bridge, the oldest surviving suspension bridge, and one of the longest suspension bridges in the country. It runs over the East River, linking Brooklyn and Manhattan. Manhattan is home to the Statue of Liberty and Ellis Island. Millions of immigrants entered the U.S. through Ellis Island from 1892 to 1954. As they sailed into New York Harbor, they were welcomed by the Statue of Liberty, a symbol of peace and freedom. Today, you can visit Ellis Island, now the Ellis Island Immigration Museum, and tour the Statue of Liberty!

Some Other Wacky New York Town Names:

Calcium
Cat Elbow Corner
Endwell
Flushing
Friendship
Handsome Eddy
Horseheads
Lava

Lawyersville
Lonelyville
North Pole
Noseville
Oniontown
Onoville
Shady

As the story goes, in 1921, **Endwell** was named for the Endwell shoe, a line of shoes manufactured by the Endicott-Johnson Shoe Company. Henry B. Endicott, a partner in the company, was a prominent man in the county. Some say he thought of the name *Endwell* by rearranging the letters in his son Wendell's name!

In the early 1800s, **Friendship** was called Fighting Corners because the people living in the hills and the people living in the valleys were always feuding. In 1815, a resident suggested they change the name to Friendship, either because the feuding had stopped, or in the hopes that it would bring peace to the community and stop discouraging people from moving there!

A meeting was held to decide on a new name for the town of Jugville. After each suggestion, residents would call out, "Oh no! Not that!" Finally, someone suggested they just call it **Onoville**!

This town is not the secret headquarters of the Caped Crusader! It was named for a nearby cave with many species of bat. The cave is also home to other animals, many of them rare, and is part of the Bat Cave Preserve. To **Bat Cave**, Robin!

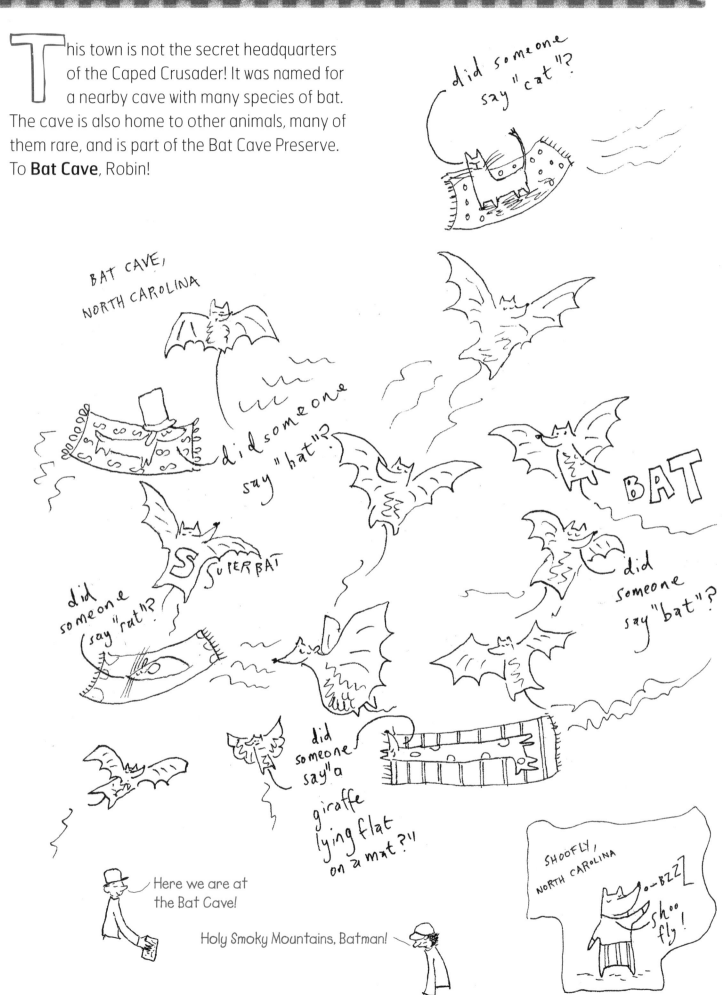

did someone say "cat"?

BAT CAVE, NORTH CAROLINA

did someone say "bat"?

BAT

SUPERBAT

did someone say "rat"?

did someone say "bat"?

did someone say "a giraffe lying flat on a mat?"

Here we are at the Bat Cave!

Holy Smoky Mountains, Batman!

SHOOFLY, NORTH CAROLINA

BZZZ shoo fly!

North Carolina

Southeastern State
12th State, Statehood 1789

Info to Know

To protect the bats and their ecosystem, the cave in Bat Cave is not open to the public. At certain times of year, however, you can join the Nature Conservancy of North Carolina on a tour of the Bat Cave Preserve, including a trip to the base of the cave system. North Carolina is also home to Kitty Hawk, where, in 1903, the Wright Brothers took the first powered airplane flight in history. It lasted only 12 seconds!

Lay of the Land

Bat Cave is located in western North Carolina. This region, known as the Mountain Region, is home to the Appalachian Mountains and includes the famous Blue Ridge Mountains and Great Smoky Mountains.

Road Trip

How would you like to zip across a gorge – literally? If you're 10 years old or older, you can sail through the air – and through different ecosystems – on a gravity-powered zip line! Soar among the trees and over the deep mountain gorges and valleys of the Nantahala National Forest, in the Great Smoky Mountains National Park!

Some Other Wacky North Carolina Town Names:

Bandana	Number 2
Cash Corner	Shoofly
Cheeks	Spies
Duck	The Black Cat
Finger	Toast
Grandfather	Vests
Meat Camp	Welcome
Micro	Worry

Bandana either got its name when a railroad worker found a suitable site for the area's railroad station and marked it with his bandana, or when a politician wearing a red bandana campaigned in the area.

In a meeting to decide on a town name, **Welcome** was finally chosen because of the general store's *Welcome* sign and because as one resident stated, "Everybody's welcome here!"

Each suggestion for a post office name submitted by Jane Elizabeth Caldwell (or some say a Mrs. Henderson) was rejected by postal authorities. Worried that none of her names would ever be chosen, she was inspired to submit **"Worry"** as a place name. No worries – it was accepted!

ZAP, NORTH DAKOTA

This town was named in 1913, but different reasons are given for why the town chose such a name. We'll *zip* through two of them! One explains that it was named for a prominent Minnesota banking family named Zapp. The other tells how Mr. Pettibone, a railroad official charged with naming new communities in the area, gave the town its name. He commented that the coal mine at the edge of town reminded him of one he had seen in Scotland (or Wales), called Zapp. To Americanize the name he dropped a "p" and zap! – it became **Zap!**

North Dakota

Midwestern State

39th State, Statehood 1889

Info to Know

Zap is located in southwestern North Dakota. When you're in the region, be sure to drive the Enchanted Highway, a 32-mile stretch of highway between the towns of Regent and Gladstone lined with funny, whimsical, metal sculptures. It's the creation of Gary Greff, a Regent resident who wanted to attract visitors to his small community. He was successful! People come from all over to photograph the incredible works of art!

Southeast of Zap is Bismarck, the capital of North Dakota. In 1804, in their journey to explore the Louisiana Territory, Lewis and Clark camped near a Hidatsa-Mandan Indian village near Bismarck. There they met Sacagawea, who joined the two explorers and helped them in their expedition across western North America.

Lay of the Land

North Dakota's Badlands region with its unique rock formations is in the southwestern part of the state. There you'll find Theodore Roosevelt National Park, named for the 26th president, Theodore Roosevelt, who loved spending time in the Badlands. A favorite activity in the park is wildlife viewing. Visitors can spot a range of Great Plains wildlife, including bison, bighorn sheep, white-tailed deer and elk.

Road Trip

Many different Indian groups once lived in what is now North Dakota. You can experience some of American Indian culture today by stopping in Bismarck and attending one of the largest Pow Wows in the country — the United Tribes International Pow Wow, which represents more than 70 tribes. There are over 1,500 drummers and dancers and over 20,000 spectators!

Some Other Wacky North Dakota Town Names:

Antler
Bachelor
Baker
Cando
Cannon Ball
Concrete
Fried

Huff
Overly
Pillsbury
Rugby
Tokio
Wild Rice

In 1884, county commissioner Prosper Parker led his commission in choosing a town as county seat of Towner County. When others questioned the commission's authority, Parker retorted, "We can do it." To prove it, he named the town **Cando**!

Cannon Ball got its name from the numerous cannonball-shaped boulders found in a nearby stream.

Wild Rice was named for a stream, which got its name from the wild rice that grew on its banks.

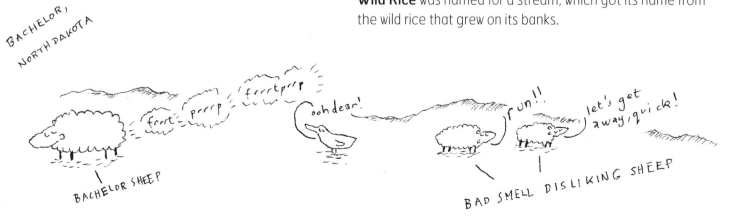

BACHELOR SHEEP

ooh dear!

run!!

let's get away, quick!

BAD SMELL DISLIKING SHEEP

GETAWAY, OHIO

Hey, come back here! No need to take this place name so literally! But what *is* its origin? It depends on who you ask! Some explain that before the village was named **Getaway**, it was called Russell's Place, for resident Francis Russell. Russell owned a general store, blacksmith, and mill, which drew people from miles around. The visitors often told Russell their woes, to which he'd respond, "Getaway," meaning *You don't say!* This prompted them to call Russell, and eventually the village, "Getaway."

Another story tells that in around 1870, a resident was building a fence when a stranger approached. Mocking the small village, the stranger asked, "What's the name of this *city*?" The insulted resident replied, "Get away!" Still others explain that this area was a meeting point for slaves escaping from the slave states of Kentucky and West Virginia to the free state of Ohio. From this point, later referred to as "The Getaway Point," and then "Getaway," they were helped by the Underground Railroad to get to Macedonia, Ohio, where they were safe from capture by former masters and slave hunters.

BLOOMERTOWN, OHIO

hello

hello

now showing DRAT

BLOOM ING CINEMA

Getaway is a great little getaway!

You can say that again!

74

Some Other Wacky Ohio Town Names:

Bloomertown
Brokensword
Candy Town
Celeryville
Coolville
Delightful
Dull
Fleatown

Hicksville
Kitchen
Mount Healthy
Newcomerstown
Revenge
Tobasco
Veto

Coolville was named for Simeon Cooley, the father of an early settler, while **Dull** was named after a J.M. Dull, one of the town's leading citizens.

Veto honors Judge Ephraim Cutler, who, in 1802, at the Ohio Constitutional Convention, vetoed a clause in the constitution that would have allowed slavery in the soon-to-be state of Ohio.

Originally called Mount Pleasant, **Mount Healthy** got its name in the 1850s, when the community escaped a cholera epidemic.

TABASCO, OHIO

Ohio
Midwestern State
17th State, Statehood 1803

Info to Know

Cincinnati, in southwestern Ohio, was once a major hub of Underground Railroad activity. Today it is home to the National Underground Railroad Freedom Center. This museum uses storytelling, role-playing, and hands-on activities to help visitors learn about slavery and the struggle for freedom in the past and present.

Lay of the Land

Ohio is bordered by Lake Erie to the north and the Ohio River to the south. Lake Erie has 24 islands. One of the largest is Kelleys Island, famous for its glacial grooves — long grooves in limestone bedrock, carved out by ancient glacier ice. Along the Ohio River is a flood wall, built to protect against flooding. In the city of Portsmouth, the wall is decorated with beautiful murals illustrating the history of the Portsmouth area.

Road Trip

Head over to Cleveland, the second largest city in Ohio, on the shores of Lake Erie. There's lots to do there, but perhaps its most popular site is the Rock and Roll Hall of Fame and Museum, which celebrates — you guessed it — rock and roll! Giant colorful guitars greet you outside the impressive building. Once inside, you're bombarded with rock and roll memorabilia, from costumes and instruments of rock stars, to their rejection letters from record companies. Grab a pair of headphones and listen to your favorite tunes. Watch the films and videos. By the time you leave, you'll be an expert on the past, present, and future of rock and roll!

BOWLEGS, OKLAHOMA

Y ou say this town was named for a horse-riding cowboy? Well, you don't have a leg to stand on! The legendary Seminole Indian chief, Hollate Mekko, was known by white settlers as Billy Bowlegs. Some suggest the town was named in honor of Billy Bowlegs or his granddaughter Lizzie Bowlegs, after oil was found on her land. But it seems it was actually named in memory of Billy's grandson Dave and Dave's family, after they were killed in their home in 1913, in what is now the town of **Bowlegs**.

BOWLEGS, OKLAHOMA

There's so much to do around these parts, it'll bowl you over!

Well, then. Let's shake a leg!

BRIGHT bow CAFÉ

Oklahoma

Southwestern State
46th State, Statehood 1907

Info to Know

In 1858, as part of the Indian Removal Act, the Seminoles, led by Bowlegs, were relocated from Florida to Indian Territory, now Oklahoma. This journey later became known as the Trail of Tears. The Trail of Tears was a journey American Indians were forced to take by the United States government in the mid-1800s. They had to leave their lands in the southeastern U.S. and move west to Indian Territory. The journey was called the Trail of Tears because it was very long and difficult, and thousands died along the way.

In 1889, tens of thousands of people took part in a race for land, called a land run. The United States opened two million acres of Indian Territory to settlers, on a first-come, first-served basis. Settlers lined up on the border, and when a gun went off at noon on April 22, the frenzied rush began. Some cheated, sneaking in early to make their claims. They became known as "Sooners," and Oklahoma became known as the Sooner State!

Lay of the Land

What substance is found in the earth throughout Oklahoma? Oil! Oil flows from thousands of wells across the state. Even the state's Capitol Building is surrounded by working oil wells. Perhaps most known for its oil is Tulsa, in the state's northeast region. After oil was discovered there in 1901, people began flooding the area, with new towns springing up overnight. More and more oil was discovered in the 1900s, and for a number of decades, Tulsa was known as the "Oil Capital of the World"! To learn more about the state's oil history, visit the Oklahoma Oil Museum, in central Oklahoma.

Road Trip

You can visit the Oklahoma Land Run Monument, in Oklahoma City, where larger-than-life-sized bronze sculptures depict the 1889 land run. This huge monument includes sun-bonneted women, cowboys, horses, and wagons, all in a race for land. It's a work in progress, but once completed, it will include 45 individual sculptures, each telling its own story. At 365 feet in length, it will be one of the largest free-standing bronze sculptures in the world! Also in Oklahoma City is the annual Red Earth Native American Cultural Festival, the largest festival of its kind, where you'll see American Indian crafts, dances, and a parade of more than 100 tribes marching in full regalia! And for a taste of cowboy life, take part in the annual Chuck Wagon Gathering and Children's Cowboy Festival!

Some Other Wacky Oklahoma Town Names:

Battiest	Gene Autry	Okay
Bugtussle	Grainola	Paw Paw
Bushyhead	Hydro	Peek
Cookietown	Non	Sunkist
Fame	Nuyaka	Titanic

Bushyhead was named for Cherokee chief Dennis W. Bushyhead.

The town of **Gene Autry** was originally named Lou, then Dresden, then Berwyn! But when Gene Autry, the famous singing cowboy and Western movie star, bought the Flying A Ranch on the west edge of Berwyn in 1938, the town changed its name once again, to Gene Autry! The town is also home to the Gene Autry Oklahoma Museum.

Okay was not named for the initials of the state, as you might have thought, but for the OK Truck Manufacturing Company.

no, I think it's custard

oil?

oil flows from thousands of wells across the state

SISTERS, OREGON BROTHERS, OREGON

Meet the Three Sisters. No, they're not a singing group, nor some pesky neighbors. They're three beautiful peaks in the Cascade Mountain Range, called Faith, Hope, and Charity, or the Three Sisters. What would you name a town with a great view of these peaks? Why, **Sisters**, or course! The town got its name in 1888.

Don't feel left out, boys! Oregon also has a town called **Brothers**! One reason given is that a homesteader was looking out at the beautiful peaks when he noticed three hills nearby, southeast of the Three Sisters. He called them the Three Brothers. And so, in 1913, the town got its name. Another explanation is that among its early settlers were many bands, or groups, of brothers.

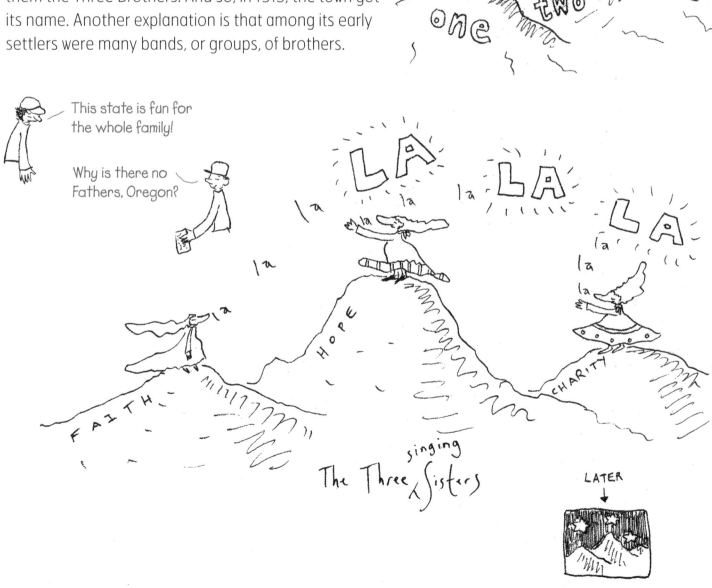

brothers ARE We

one two three

This state is fun for the whole family!

Why is there no Fathers, Oregon?

LA LA LA

FAITH   HOPE   CHARITY

The Three singing Sisters

LATER

Some Other Wacky Oregon Town Names:

Aloha
Arock
Boring
Bridal Veil
Drain
Grizzly
Lookingglass
Mohawk

Paisley
Powers
Remote
Sweet Home
Talent
Wagontire
Zigzag

The story behind **Boring** is a little...well...boring! Established in 1903, the community was named for long-time resident W.H. Boring.

Remote is a small, remote town.

Zigzag has a zigzagging road leading to it.

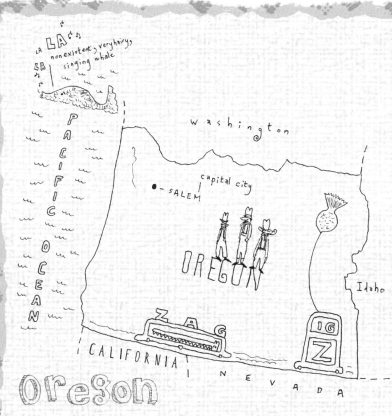

Oregon

Western State
33rd State, Statehood 1859

Info to Know

Sisters is a scenic town with lots to do. Two of its annual events are a rodeo and an outdoor quilt show. The Cascade Mountain Range is located in western North America. It stretches from southern British Columbia in Canada, to Washington, Oregon, and Northern California. It is part of the Ring of Fire, a circle of volcanoes surrounding the basin of the Pacific Ocean.

Lay of the Land

If you like mountains, try horseback riding in the Eagle Cap Wilderness, in the heart of the Wallowa Mountains in northeastern Oregon, or go sledding on Mount Hood, the largest mountain in the state, and the fourth largest in the Cascade Range. For an incredible lake, move on to southern Oregon, to Crater Lake, the deepest lake in the country. Known for its deep blue color, it was formed in the mouth of a collapsed volcano!

Road Trip

Make your way to western Oregon to visit Sea Lion Caves, a huge natural sea cave (the world's largest), home to Stellar sea lions and sea birds. You'll watch hordes of wild sea lions resting and playing on sea cliff rocks and jumping in and out of the water! While in the region, visit the Oregon Dunes, along the coast, where you can travel across miles of windswept sand in a giant dune buggy!

BIRD-IN-HAND, PENNSYLVANIA

This community got its name when people "saw the sign"! The village of **Bird-in-Hand** was named for a Colonial-era inn. The inn had a swinging sign in front, with a painting of a bird perched in a hand and the saying "A bird in the hand is worth two in the bush" (meaning it's better to be happy with what you have, than to try to get more and risk losing everything). Many say that the original sign was a bit different, showing a man with a bird in his hand and two birds perched in a bush.

And how did the inn get its unusual name? When a road was being built between Lancaster and Philadelphia, two road surveyors found themselves in the area after a day's work. While discussing whether to sleep there for the night or go back to Lancaster, they remembered the old adage "A bird in the hand is worth two in the bush" and decided to stay!

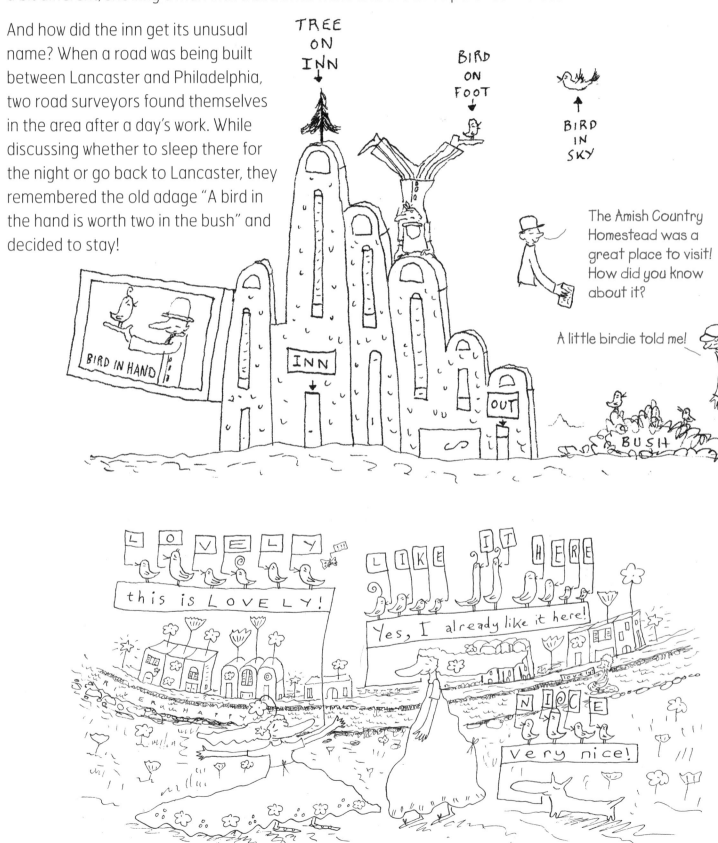

TREE ON INN

BIRD ON FOOT

BIRD IN SKY

BIRD IN HAND

INN

OUT

The Amish Country Homestead was a great place to visit! How did you know about it?

A little birdie told me!

BUSH

LOVELY

this is LOVELY!

LIKE IT HERE

Yes, I already like it here!

NICE

very nice!

Pennsylvania

Northeastern State
2nd State, Statehood 1787

Info to Know

Bird-in-Hand wasn't the only community named for an inn sign. As America grew, and more people traveled by covered wagon or stagecoach for long stretches of time, inns, each with its own unique sign, grew along the roads. These signs had pictures on them, so people who couldn't read English or couldn't read at all would be able to identify them. The towns that grew up around these signs took on the names of the inns.

Lay of the Land

Lancaster County, often called Amish Country, is home to many Amish communities, including the oldest Amish community in the United States. The Amish are a religious group that does not use modern-day conveniences, in order to preserve its traditions. The Amish travel by horse-drawn carriages instead of cars, and have their own style of dress. Around four million people visit the beautiful, quiet neighborhoods of Lancaster County each year. Bird-in-Hand is one of these neighborhoods. It has quaint country roads, one-room schoolhouses, and horse-drawn carriages. It also has antique shops, a farmer's market, miniature golf, and balloon rides.

Road Trip

Philadelphia played a major role in America's move toward independence. It is home to the Liberty Bell and Declaration of Independence. It is the city where the United States Constitution was signed. Visit the Liberty Bell Center to view the Liberty Bell and learn about its history, Independence Hall, where Thomas Jefferson drafted the Declaration of Independence, and the National Constitution Center, a museum that teaches about the U.S. Constitution through multimedia exhibits. A highlight of the National Constitution Center is Signers' Hall, where you can walk among life-sized bronze statues of John Hancock, George Washington, Benjamin Franklin, and other signers of the Declaration of Independence!

Some Other Wacky Pennsylvania Town Names:

Compass
Coupon
Cracker Jack
Darling
Eighty Four
Fearnot
Library
Live Easy
Lovely
Mars
Panic
Presto
Rough and Ready
Tallyho
Tuna

Compass was also named for an inn sign — one with a picture of a sailor's compass.

Many say **Eighty Four** was so named because its post office was established in 1884. Others say its name originates from a time when postal workers threw mailbags from trains. The drop-off location of this community was known as "Drop 84."

Darling was named for Jesse Darlington, the first postmaster. Darlington was already taken.

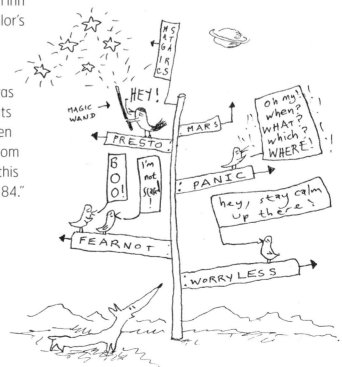

HOG ISLAND, RHODE ISLAND

Hog Island is a small island in Narragansett Bay. Early settlers found it to be a convenient place for keeping hogs (and other livestock) because the surrounding water kept them from wandering off the island; they didn't even need fences! This natural barrier also kept predators, like foxes and wolves, from getting to the hogs and other animals on the island. And that's not hogwash!

HOG ISLAND RHODE ISLAND

"I am a hog who stands at the edge of the sea and snorts and sniffs and snorts some more and dreams about sailing away..."

HOG ISLAND · RHODE ISLAND

"I am a fox who stands at the edge of the mainland and sighs foxily and dreams about sailing away..."

HOG 'N' FOX

There's so much to do in this area! Let's go fishing, sailing, kayaking, see a lighthouse, take a ferry ride...

Whoa! No need to go hog wild!

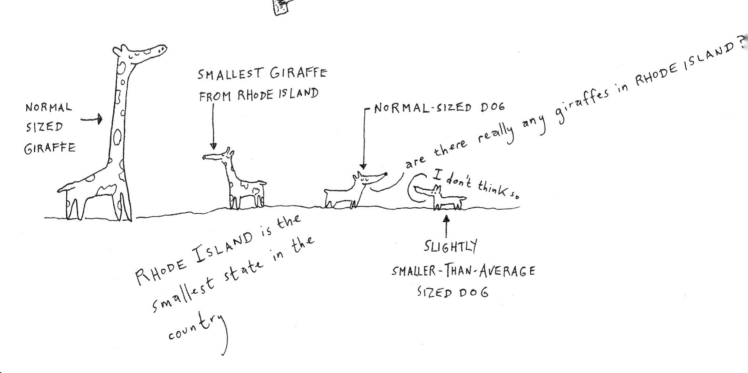

NORMAL SIZED GIRAFFE

SMALLEST GIRAFFE FROM RHODE ISLAND

NORMAL-SIZED DOG

are there really any giraffes in RHODE ISLAND?

I don't think so.

RHODE ISLAND is the smallest state in the country

SLIGHTLY SMALLER-THAN-AVERAGE SIZED DOG

Rhode Island

Northeastern State
13th State, Statehood 1790

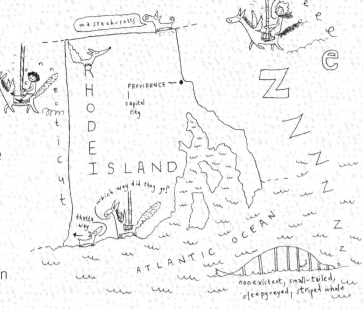

Info to Know

Hog Island sits at the entrance to the harbor of Bristol, Rhode Island. Bristol is home to the oldest continuously-celebrated Fourth of July celebration in the nation, having celebrated every year since 1785! The festivities begin as early as June 14th (Flag Day), with activities like outdoor concerts, soapbox races, and firefighter competitions. On July 4th, the town holds the oldest annual parade in the United States. Bristol has been nicknamed "America's Most Patriotic Town." In fact, instead of the usual yellow line running down the middle of a road, Bristol's main street has center stripes of red, white, and blue!

Lay of the Land

Rhode Island is the smallest state in the country – only 48 miles long and 37 miles wide. Despite its name, Rhode Island is not an island, though it does have a shoreline dotted with islets (small islands) and beaches.

The East Bay Bike Path is a scenic bike path running from Bristol to Providence. The trail follows an old abandoned railway and offers spectacular views of Narragansett Bay. Providence is the capital of Rhode Island and its most populated city. Established in 1636, it is the oldest settlement in Rhode Island, and one of the first cities established in the United States. Newport is another major Rhode Island city. It's home to many mansions and to the International Tennis Hall of Fame!

Road Trip

Make your way over to Westerly, in the southwest corner of the state, along the shores of the Atlantic Ocean. There you can visit the Flying Horse Carousel – the oldest continuously-operated carousel in the country. Unlike other carousels, these horses aren't attached to the floor; they're hung by chains. The faster the carousel turns, the farther out the horses swing, making you feel like you're flying! Each horse is hand carved from a single piece of wood, and saddles are made from real leather.

Some Other Wacky Rhode Island Town Names:

Arctic
Moosup Valley
Nooseneck
Prudence
Quidnick

Quonochontaug
Rice City
Snug Harbor
Watch Hill
Woonsocket

Some say **Nooseneck** got its name because each fall the Narragansett Indians would come to the area to catch deer by using nooses hung from birch trees. Others explain that Nooseneck is derived from an Algonquian word meaning "place of the beaver."

Prudence was named for the island on which it's found. The island was one of three that Rhode Island founder, Roger Williams, bought from the Indians in Narragansett Bay. He named each island for a different virtue: Hope, Patience, and Prudence.

Many explain that **Watch Hill** was a strategic lookout point for colonists during the French and Indian War and the Revolutionary War. The Niantic Indians, who lived there earlier – in the 1600s – probably also used it as a lookout point.

PUMPKINTOWN, SOUTH CAROLINA

It's agreed that this community got its name from the hundreds of giant-sized pumpkins growing in the area. But the details vary depending on which story you hear. According to one, in the 1700s, a trader spent the night at an inn belonging to the land's owner, William Sutherland. The trader told Sutherland that if it were up to him, he'd call the place Pumpkintown. Sutherland must have loved the name, because **Pumpkintown** it became! The other story tells how Cornelius Keith was the land's first white settler, and a community grew up on his land. One day, settlers were arguing over what to name the community, when a resident got up and waved his arms around, gesturing toward the pumpkin-filled valley. "Men," he yelled, "jest quit arguin' 'bout the whole thing and call 'er Pumpkin Town!" So they did!

Some Other Wacky South Carolina Town Names:

Coward
Cowpens
Due West
Fingerville
Frogmore
Limp
Lucknow
Nine Times

Old House
Quicktown
Rains
Round O
South of the Border
Spiderweb
Trio

Rains, South Carolina

Nine Times got its name because a Cherokee trade path crossed a stream in the area nine times.

As the story goes, **Rains** was so named because during the construction of a railroad here in 1941, it rained and rained for days.

According to legend, **Round O** got its name after a meeting between English settlers and American Indians was held in this area, and one of the Indians had a big O painted on his chest (or some say shoulder).

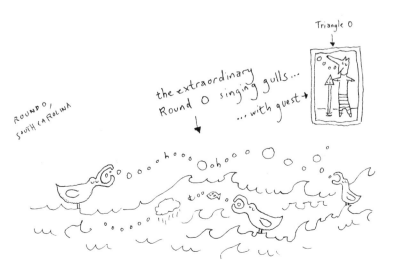

South Carolina

Southeastern State
8th State, Statehood 1788

Info to Know

On the second Saturday in October, Pumpkintown holds its annual Pumpkin Festival, with homemade crafts, food – including pumpkin butter – and entertainment, such as a greased-pole climb, parade, and quilt raffle. There's also clogging and bluegrass music. About 30,000 people attend the festival each year.

Lay of the Land

Near Pumpkintown is Table Rock State Park, at the edge of the Blue Ridge Mountains in northwest South Carolina. The park has lakes and hiking trails and is home to Pinnacle Mountain, the tallest peak lying within the state of South Carolina. (Nearby Sassafras Mountain is taller, but its peak actually lies in North Carolina.) Hike Table Rock Mountain to see its dramatic cliffs and incredible views.

Road Trip

The city of Charleston, in South Carolina's south, is one of America's most historic cities and houses the oldest gardens in the country. People from around the world visit the Magnolia Plantation and Gardens, with its magnificent gardens, swamp, nature train, boat tours, petting zoo and nature center. They also come to tour the plantation house and slave cabins, to learn about the history of African-American life at Magnolia.

WOUNDED KNEE, SOUTH DAKOTA

You want to know why this town is called **Wounded Knee**? Well, I guess it never hurts to ask! It was named after an incident in which a Sioux Indian was wounded in the knee. One story tells how he was wounded in a battle against a band of Crow Indians. Another tells how he and a friend were in love with the same woman. In an attempt to make him less desirable to the woman, his friend shot an arrow through his knee. Both stories take place on the banks of a creek, also called Wounded Knee. Many say the town was named for the creek.

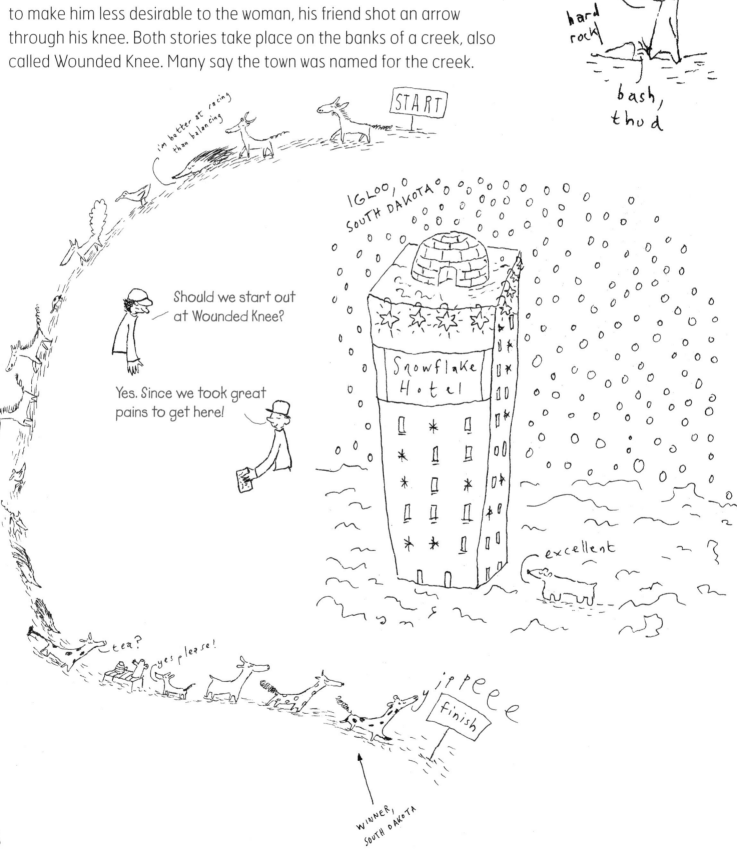

WOUNDED KNEE, SOUTH DAKOTA

OW!

hard rock

bash, thud

i'm better at racing than balancing

START

IGLOO, SOUTH DAKOTA

Snowflake Hotel

excellent

Should we start out at Wounded Knee?

Yes. Since we took great pains to get here!

tea?

yes please!

yippeee

finish

WINNER, SOUTH DAKOTA

86

South Dakota

Midwestern State
40th State, Statehood 1889

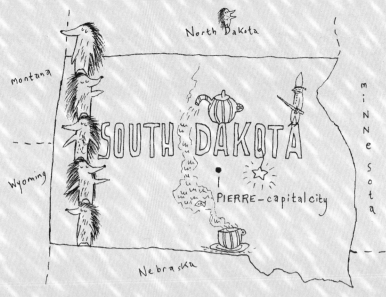

Info to Know

In 1890, the U.S. Calvary killed 300 Lakota Sioux Indians at Wounded Knee Creek, in what has become known as the Wounded Knee Massacre. You can visit the massacre site and memorial in Wounded Knee, and to learn more about this tragic event, visit the Wounded Knee Museum, in Wall, about 90 miles north of Wounded Knee. This incident is considered the last major armed conflict between U.S. troops and American Indians.

Lay of the Land

Wounded Knee is located in South Dakota's Western Region, also called the Black Hills, Badlands, and Lakes Region. This is where you'll find Badlands National Park, with its views of fantastic rock formations — spires and pinnacles, ridges, canyons, buttes, and gorges, in purples, yellows, reds, oranges, tans, grays, and whites. These formations are caused by erosion, the wearing away of rock by wind and water. The park is also famous for the numerous fossils found there. A variety of fossilized animals have been discovered, from sea creatures to mammals, and more fossils continue to be excavated. But the Badlands National Park is not all rock. It's also home to the largest protected mixed-grass prairie in the United States.

Road Trip

In the Black Hills, you'll find two incredible sculptures, Mount Rushmore National Monument and Crazy Horse Memorial. Mount Rushmore features the faces of U.S. presidents Washington, Jefferson, Lincoln, and Roosevelt, carved into a granite mountain. Each face is 60 feet tall and was chiseled out of the mountain using dynamite and jackhammers. Mount Rushmore is visited by more than two million people each year. Crazy Horse Memorial is a work in progress. When completed, it will be the largest mountain carving in the world, and will feature Crazy Horse, a famous Lakota chief, riding his horse. The face of Crazy Horse is complete. Work is now being done on the horse's head. When you visit the site, you might even catch the workers dynamiting the mountain! While there, be sure to visit the Crazy Horse Memorial complex, which includes the Indian Museum of North America and the Native American Cultural Center.

Some Other Wacky South Dakota Town Names:

Blunt
Chance
Fedora
Hammer
Hitchcock
Ideal
Igloo
Interior
Kidder
Parade
Porcupine
Pringle
Red Shirt
Tea
Winner

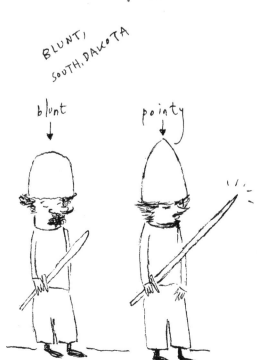

Fedora was either named for the wife of a railroad clerk, or for the fedora hat, which was a popular item at a local store.

Parade was originally called Paradis, for George Paradis. But since there already was a Paradis, South Dakota, residents changed the name's ending, making it Parade!

Different stories are told about the naming of **Tea**. According to one, it resulted from a town meeting about the name, after someone yelled out, "Tea time!" According to another, when some residents suggested naming the village Beer, others rejected it, suggesting Tea instead, since it was an alternative, more respectable drink!

The stories behind the naming of **Yum Yum** aren't especially sweet, but at least they're not in bad taste! In the late 1800s, when general store owner John Garnett wanted his community to get a post office, he had to quickly come up with a name, and Yum Yum popped into his head. It was the name of a popular brand of cookies (or some say candy kisses) that he sold in his general store. He figured it would be a one-of-a-kind name, and he sure was right! According to another source, the community was named for the character of Yum-Yum in Gilbert and Sullivan's opera, *The Mikado*, which opened in 1885.

We're in Yum Yum!

Hoo Hoo!

No, that's in West Virginia!

YUM YUM, TENNESSEE

THE STORY OF THE MIKADO

NOW SHOWING at YUM YUM theatre

W.S. GILBERT

from an old MIKADO POSTER

looks good!

let's see it!

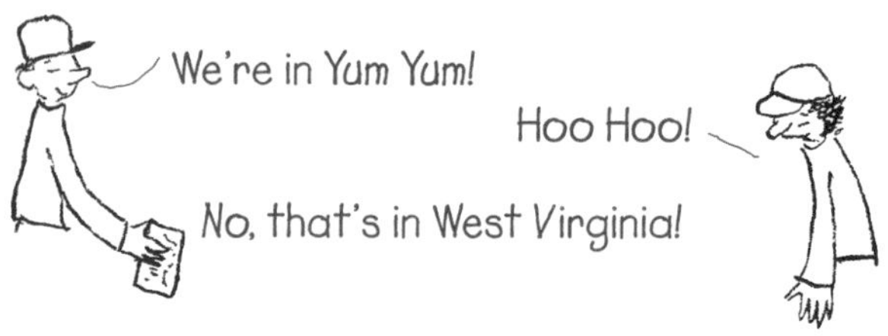

CHATTANOOGA, TENNESSEE

bye bye valley

hello hill

cheep cheep

hello steep

the steepest passenger railway in the world

TOPSY, TENNESSEE

Tennessee

Southeastern State
12th State, Statehood 1789

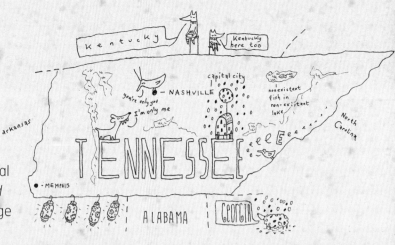

Info to Know

Nashville, the capital of Tennessee, is known as the capital of country music. Nashville is home to the famous *Grand Ole Opry*, a weekly country music radio program and stage concert broadcast from the Grand Ole Opry House. You can also visit the nearby Grand Ole Opry Museum, and the Country Music Hall of Fame and Museum.

Lay of the Land

Yum Yum is located in southwestern Tennessee. While you're in the region, stop in Memphis, Tennessee's largest city. Memphis sits in the southwestern corner of the state on the banks of the Mississippi River. In Memphis you'll find the Rock 'n' Roll Soul Museum, where you'll learn about the birth of rock and soul music. You'll also find Graceland, the mansion and estate of Elvis Presley, now a museum. And visit the National Civil Rights Museum, housed in what was once the Lorraine Motel, where Martin Luther King Jr. was assassinated.

Road Trip

Another great city in Tennessee is Chattanooga, in the southeastern part of the state. Among its many sites and attractions is Lookout Mountain. To get to the top, ride the Lookout Mountain Incline Railway – the steepest passenger railway in the world! Enjoy the panoramic views along the way, and stop at the Civil War sites at the top of the mountain. When you're done, travel about two miles north to Ruby Falls, a natural underground waterfall! And for another underground adventure, head to Sweetwater, where you can take a boat ride in the Lost Sea, America's largest underground lake!

Some Other Wacky Tennessee Town Names:

Bitter End
Campaign
Defeated
Difficult
Dismal
Finger
Friendsville
Frog Jump
Mascot
Only
Ozone
Skullbone
Spot
Topsy
Worry

Difficult was really supposed to be called Williams Crossroad, but whoever wrote "Williams Crossroads" on the post office application had messy handwriting. Unable to decipher the name, a postal worker scrawled "This is difficult" over it, causing postal officials to think the community's name was *Difficult*! Others say it was difficult to climb the steep hill leading to the community. Still others say a Civil War battle was taking place in the area, and a group of Union soldiers were having a hard time navigating through the heavily wooded terrain. Someone informed their general that the area in which the soldiers were encamped was *difficult*. His response? "Get to Difficult and find them!"

When the town of Dreamer needed a new name, **Only** was chosen. Some explain that Only was the only name like it! Others say an early settler ran a general store, and when asked the price of an item, he would always answer, "It's only ten cents," or "It's only a dollar," etc. Residents began calling it the Only store, and they called their town Only too!

In 1901, some residents had gathered outside their town's general store, discussing what to name their new post office. Will Lafferty rode by on his mule and jokingly suggested they name the post office for **Topsy** – his mule! So they did!

Well I'm the only two-haired bird in ONLY!

I'm the only three-toothed dog in ONLY

I'm only a normal ladybug

TELEPHONE, TEXAS

Around 1886, Pete Hindman, owner of the community's general store, wanted to open a post office. To apply for one, he had to come up with a name. But each of Hindman's suggestions were rejected, putting his plans for a post office on hold — until a bell went off in his head! Hindman's store had the only telephone in town, so he suggested the name **Telephone**. It was a great call!

TELEPHONE, TEXAS

I'm hung up on Telephone and other Texas towns!

I hear you! I can hang up my hat in a state like this.

PARKING

Some famous (and not-so-famous) noodley, curly, twisty, twirly landmarks:

NOODLE CREEK

I ♡ cheese

MACARONI MOUNTAIN

SPAGHETTI LAKE

FORK-SHAPED TOOTH

STATUE OF THE WORLD'S MOST FAMOUS NOODLE-EATING DOG

CURLY-CRESTED PIGEON

Some Other Wacky Texas Town Names:

Big Foot	Necessity
Cash	Noodle
Exray	Notrees
Goodnight	Oatmeal
Jolly	Pancake
Jot 'Em Down	Smiley
Looneyville	Uncertain
Mudville	

Goodnight, **Jolly**, **Looneyville**, and **Pancake** were all named after residents of their towns. This includes rancher Charles Goodnight, rancher and farmer W.H. Jolly, storeowner John Looney, and postmaster John R. Pancake! There is also a community named Cash, which honors storeowner John A. Money!

When applying for a post office in 1893, residents of a town in north central Texas wanted to stress to postal officials that for them, a post office was a necessity. So they submitted the name **Necessity**!

Noodle was named for a creek that twists and turns like a noodle.

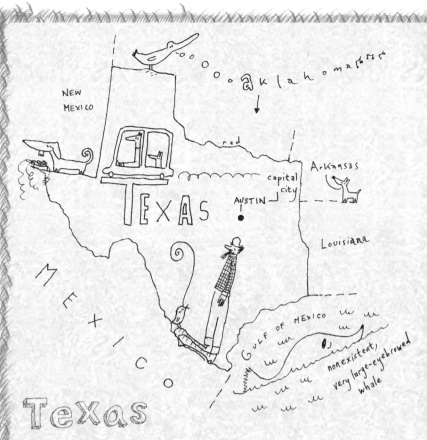

Texas

Southwestern State
28th State, Statehood 1845

Info to Know

Interestingly, there is also a Telegraph, Texas! Before the telephone was invented, people used the telegraph to communicate over long distances. The telegraph sent a code – called Morse code – of long and short electric currents, each of which stood for different letters, along wires crossing the country. Once received, the message was decoded and written down for its recipients.

Lay of the Land

The Rio Grande, one of the longest rivers in North America, forms the border between Texas and Mexico. Texas won its independence from Mexico in the 1830s, during the Texas Revolution. *Rio Grande* means "big river" in Spanish. In Mexico, the Rio Grande is known as the *Rio Bravo del Norte,* meaning "wild river of the north," or just *Rio Bravo.*

Road Trip

You can visit the Alamo, a fort in San Antonio, Texas, and the site of a famous battle during the Texas Revolution. Texas lost the battle, but the battle cry, "Remember the Alamo!" helped inspire soldiers to continue on in their fight for independence. The Alamo is one of the most visited sites in Texas. Another famous San Antonio site is the San Antonio River Walk, pathways winding along the banks of the San Antonio River, lined with cafes, galleries, shops, and attractions. You can even take a river cruise to view the exciting town and beautiful landscapes of San Antonio.

MEXICAN HAT, UTAH

Mexican Hat got its name from a nearby sandstone rock formation that looks like an upside-down sombrero! The formation is a large, disc-shaped rock, about 60 feet in diameter, resting on a much smaller base atop a rocky hill. It actually looks like the hat is balancing precariously on the hill, ready to fall off at any moment! This small community in southeast Utah is surrounded by beautiful scenery, including the San Juan River, sandstone cliffs, canyons, and sandy desert plains. Hats off to Mexican Hat!

MEXICAN HAT (CIRCUS), UTAH

What if the Mexican Hat rock formation toppled over?

It sure would give new meaning to the expression "at the drop of a hat!"

Café DES Saisons
Sunny side   Shady side

SUNNYSIDE, UTAH

SOUP

Utah

Western State
45th State, Statehood 1896

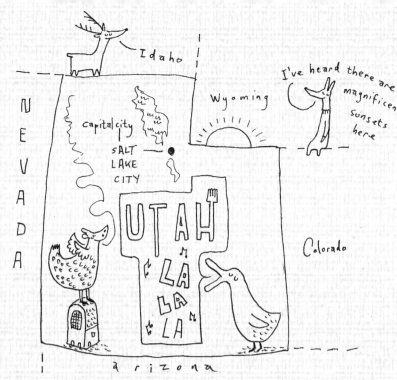

Info to Know

Not far from Mexican Hat, in Utah's southeast corner, is Four Corners, the only spot in the U.S. where four states – Utah, Colorado, New Mexico, and Arizona – meet. If you stand on the spot, marked by the flags of the four states, you'll be in four states at once!

Lay of the Land

In south central Utah, along the Utah-Arizona border, are the Coyote Buttes. The Coyote Buttes are divided into Coyote Buttes North and Coyote Buttes South. A highlight of Coyote Buttes North is a weird and spectacular rock formation called The Wave, which boasts huge twists and swirls of multicolored sandstone. The Wave was once sand dunes, which turned to rock over time. Only 20 hikers are allowed to explore The Wave each day, so as not to wear away its delicate stone. People come from around the world to photograph this stunning formation.

Road Trip

Travel to northern Utah and you'll find the famous Great Salt Lake, the largest saltwater lake in the Western Hemisphere. The lake is very salty because rivers and streams carrying salt and other minerals flow into it. Once there, much of the water evaporates, leaving the salt and minerals behind. A high concentration of salt makes waters buoyant, so it's easy to float. You can just lie on your back and relax!

A bit southeast of the Great Salt Lake is Salt Lake City, the capital and most populous city in Utah. It was founded in 1847 by a religious group of people called Latter-day Saints, or Mormons. Today, more than half the state's population is Mormon.

Some Other Wacky Utah Town Names:

American Fork
Circleville
Echo
Eggnog
Helper
Hurricane
Low
Orderville

Pickelville
Plain City
Red Wash
Spanish Fork
Sunnyside
Sunset
Whipup

Circleville is almost completely encircled by mountains and is located in a circle-shaped valley. Circleville was also home to the notorious outlaw, Butch Cassidy.

In the late 1800s, **Helper** became a railroad town and was named for the helper locomotives that *helped* pull trains up the steep inclines to Soldier Summit.

After riding down a steep hill, Mormon leader Erastus Snow (see Snowflake, Arizona) got caught in a whirlwind, which tore the top off his buggy. Snow called the hill Hurricane Hill. And the nearby town became known as **Hurricane**.

BREAD LOAF, VERMONT

Bread Loaf was named for a nearby mountain in the Green Mountain National Forest, which looks — when viewed from the north or south — like a loaf of homemade bread! I guess you can think of Bread Loaf Mountain as a real "*roll* model"!

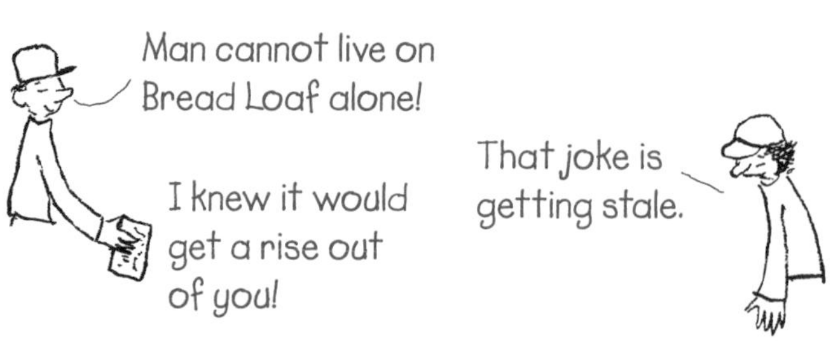

Man cannot live on Bread Loaf alone!

I knew it would get a rise out of you!

That joke is getting stale.

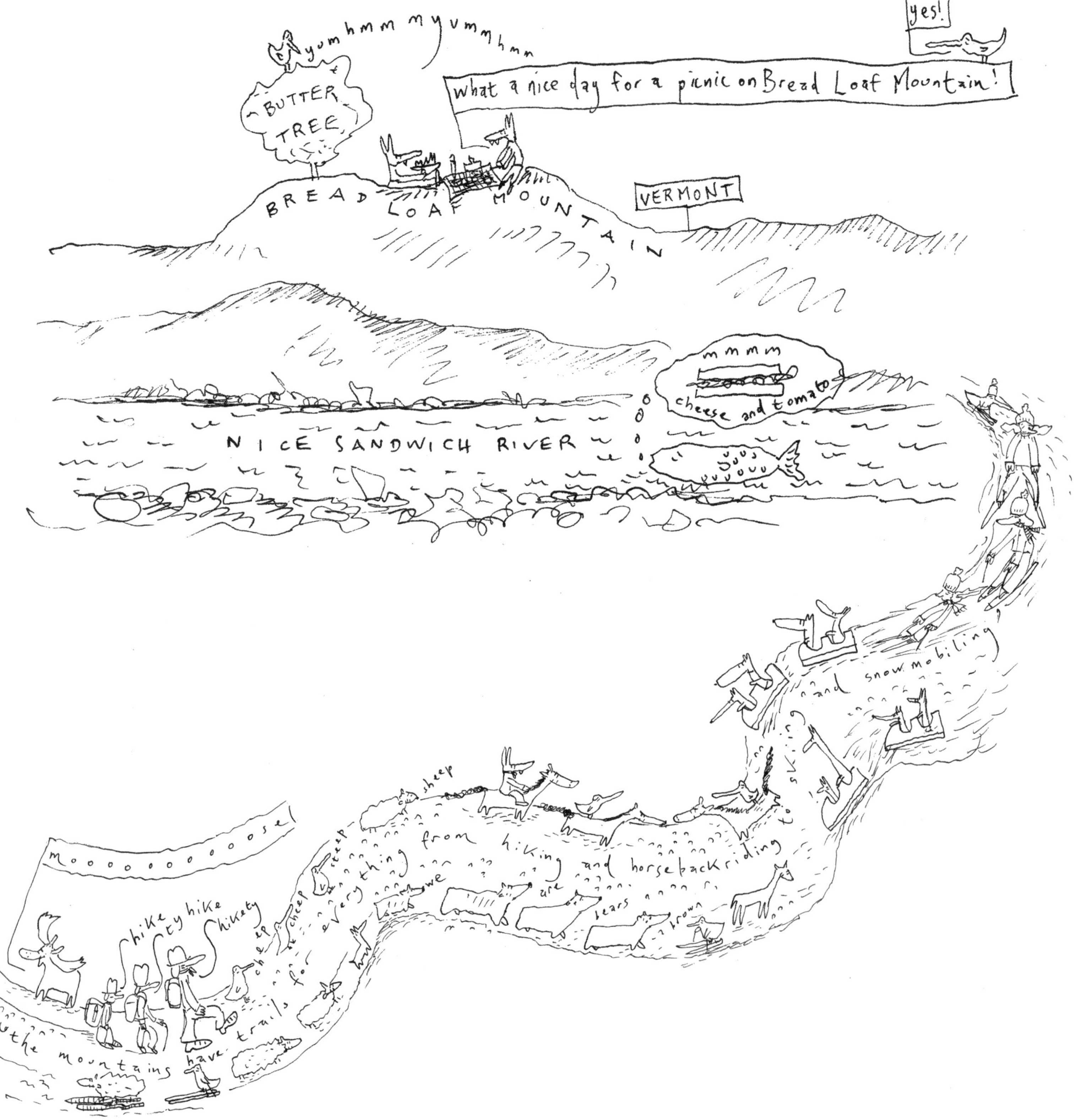

yes!

yumhmm myummhmn

BUTTER TREE

what a nice day for a picnic on Bread Loaf Mountain!

BREAD LOAF MOUNTAIN

VERMONT

mmmm cheese and tomato

NICE SANDWICH RIVER

and snowmobiling

moooooooooose!

hikey hike hikety

everything from hiking and horseback riding

the mountains have trails for

94

Some Other Wacky Vermont Town Names:

Adamant   North Hero
Chiselville   South Hero
Mosquitoville Victory

Adamant can mean stubborn or inflexible, but it can also mean "hard as a rock." The town of **Adamant** was named for the hard granite that was quarried there.

North Hero and **South Hero** – originally united and known as Two Heroes – were part of a land grant by the Republic of Vermont to Ethan Allen and hundreds of other Revolutionary War heroes, in 1779. Many believe the two of Two Heroes refers to Ethan Allen and his brother Ira. Others explain it refers to the fact that the land grant was spread across two islands.

Victory got its name during the Revolutionary War, either because its residents were praying for a victory over the British, or because they realized that victory might really be possible.

Vermont

Northeastern State
14th State, Statehood 1791

Info to Know

Many of Vermont's trees must be maple trees, because Vermont produces more maple syrup than any other state in the U.S.! Spring is maple season in Vermont, when sugar makers are out tapping maple trees to collect sap to turn into syrup. You can watch syrup being made during the Vermont Maple Open House Weekend, held at sugarhouses throughout the state!

Lay of the Land

The Green Mountain National Forest runs through southwestern and central Vermont, stretching across almost two-thirds the length of the state. Its scenery has rugged mountain peaks and beautiful Vermont villages. The mountains have trails for everything from hiking and horseback riding to skiing and snowmobiling. Many animals, including moose, black bears and white-tailed deer, make their homes here. Forests cover about 80 percent of the state.

Road Trip

There are a lot of fun factory tours in Vermont. You can start by visiting the popular Ben & Jerry's Ice Cream Factory in Waterbury, Vermont, in the Green Mountains, near the Winooski River. Continue west to Shelburne by Lake Champlain, and you'll arrive at the Vermont Teddy Bear Company, to get a behind-the-scenes look at how teddy bears are made. Travel a bit further north along the lake to tour the Lake Champlain Chocolates Factory, where you can watch the chocolate-making process and sample some of the chocolates!

CUCKOO, VIRGINIA

There's nothing **Cuckoo** about how this community got its name! In the late 1700s, there was a tavern in the area. Like many taverns of the time, it took on the name of a bird, calling itself the Cuckoo Tavern. And the community, like many communities of the time, took on the tavern's name. Local legend tells the story a little differently, explaining that the tavern got its name from the cuckoo clock – one of the first ever seen in the New World – hanging on the wall.

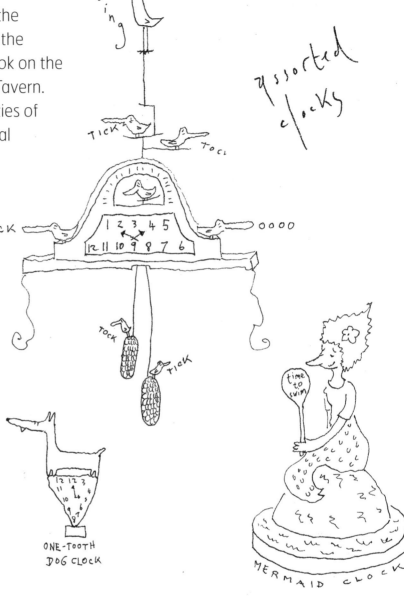

doing

assorted clocks

TICK TOCK

CUCK 0000

TOCK Tick

PONY EXPRESS CLOCK

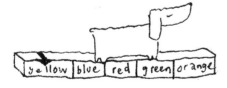

SLIGHTLY YELLOW DOG CLOCK

| yellow | blue | red | green | orange |

ONE-TOOTH DOG CLOCK

time to swim

MERMAID CLOCK

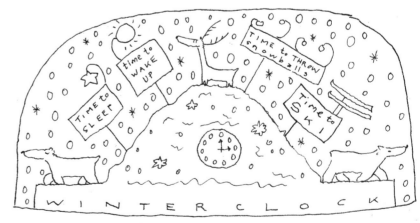

TIME to SLEEP · time to WAKE UP · TIME to THROW snowballs · Time to SKI

WINTER CLOCK

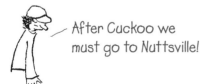

After Cuckoo we must go to Nuttsville!

And then on to Looneyville, West Virginia!

96

Virginia

Southeastern State
10th State, Statehood 1788

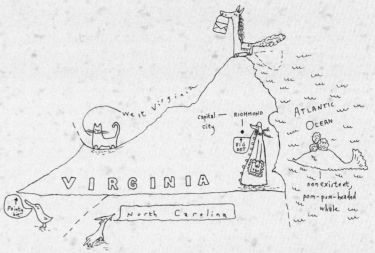

Info to Know

On June 3, 1781, patriot Jack Jouett took a daring and heroic night ride from the Cuckoo Tavern to Monticello, warning Governor Thomas Jefferson and the Virginia legislature of the approaching British army. Jouett became known as the "Paul Revere of the South!"

Lay of the Land

Cuckoo, in central Virginia, is about halfway between the cities of Richmond and Charlottesville. Richmond, southeast of Cuckoo, is the capital of Virginia and one of the state's most historic sites. In downtown Richmond you can take a boat cruise along the James River and Kanawha Canal, or stroll alongside them on the Canal Walk, where you'll learn about historic sites and personalities. In Charlottesville, northwest of Cuckoo, you can visit Thomas Jefferson's home in Monticello and tour his house, gardens and plantation.

Road Trip

You won't want to miss Virginia's historic triangle, formed by the three colonial towns of Williamsburg, Jamestown and Yorktown, in southeast Virginia by the Chesapeake Bay and James River. In Colonial Williamsburg, the world's largest living history museum, you'll feel like you've gone back in time with people, buildings, and streets looking just like they did in the 18th century! Watch blacksmiths and cabinet makers at work, marching drummer boys, and entertaining performances related to colonial days.

Some Other Wacky Virginia Town Names:

Bland	Nuttsville
Fractionville	Onemo
Fries	Ordinary
Goose Pimple	Oyster
Hurt	Stinking Point
Junction	Ticktown
Modest Town	Tiptop
Mouth of Wilson	Uno

Goose Pimple Junction was named for a couple of squabbling residents, whose arguments gave the neighbors goose pimples!

According to local legend, **Modest Town** got its name in the 1880s, from two prim and proper women who ran a boarding house in the area that also served as a stagecoach stop and post office. The women had very strict rules, which required guests to behave properly and modestly.

As the story goes, Mathews County already had many post offices, but residents of a certain hamlet wanted "one more," and when they got it, they named it **Onemo!**

some interesting architectural designs in FRACTIONVILLE

DUSTY, WASHINGTON

As the story goes, Homer Allen, the first postmaster of this community in southeast Washington, was filling out an application for a town name in 1898. Many communities were named for their postmaster, and Homer wanted this one to be named for him. But his wife, Anna Stenson, had other ideas. Life in the area was windy and dusty, and she wanted a name that would let everyone know it. So as Homer filled out the application, Anna intervened, and when the dust finally settled, **Dusty** had left all other names...in the dust!

Some Other Wacky Washington Town Names:

Aloha	Starbuck
Cashmere	Stuck
Cashup	Tumtum
Electric City	Voltage
Electron	
Forks	
Gold Bar	
Mold	
Opportunity	
Shine	
Soap Lake	

Cashup was named for a merchant whom people called "Cashup Davis." He received the nickname because he wouldn't let people buy on credit. They had to pay cash up front!

Electric City was named for the nearby Grand Coulee Dam, which generates electric power.

Some explain that **Soap Lake** is derived from *Smokiam,* the name of a nearby lake. Smokiam is an American Indian word meaning "healing waters." The lake got its name from its mineral-rich waters and creamy black mud, which were known for their healing properties. Another explanation is that as the wind blew the lake's mineral-rich water, sudsy foam formed by the shore.

Washington

Western State
42ⁿᵈ State, Statehood 1889

Info to Know

Also in southeast Washington is the city of Walla Walla (an American Indian name meaning "many waters"). There, you can visit the Fort Walla Walla Museum. Fort Walla Walla – originally Fort Nez Perce – a U.S. military post, was one of the main stops on the Oregon Trail. The museum has a pioneer village and living history performances, where people dress and act like historical figures, to show what life was like in the West in the 1800s.

Lay of the Land

The Cascade Range is a major mountain range in Washington. Many of the range's tallest peaks are volcanoes, including Mount Rainier, the range's highest peak. Mount Rainier has many layers of hardened lava and volcanic ash and is covered with snow, ice and glaciers. It also has glacier caves, caves formed within the ice of a glacier.

Road Trip

Visit Washington's famous landmark, the Space Needle, a uniquely-designed tower located in Seattle, Washington's largest city. Ride the elevator 520 feet up to the flying-saucer-shaped observation deck and get great views of downtown Seattle, the Cascade Mountains, Mount Rainier, the Olympic Mountains, surrounding islands, and more! Another fun Washington activity is cherry picking! You can pick cherries all around the state. It's no wonder Washington is among the top cherry growers in the country!

Strange as it seems, residents wanted an odd name for their community, so they decided to name it **Odd**! According to another story, residents met to decide on a town name. After many ideas were tossed around, one resident made a suggestion, which another called "odd." Oddly enough, the comment inspired the group to name their community Odd! Now what are the odds of that?

Some Other Wacky West Virginia Town Names:

Auto	Kermit
Big Ugly	Left Hand
Cinderella	Needmore
Crum	Pinch
Cucumber	Tango
Droop	Thursday
HooHoo	Uneeda
Joker	

Kermit has nothing to do with a friendly green puppet! This town was named for Kermit Roosevelt, son of the 26th U.S. President, Theodore Roosevelt.

Thursday was named by accident! In 1922, a boy filled out an application for a post office for his community. When he saw a blank line, instead of writing in the suggested town name, he wrote the day of the week, which was Thursday!

Uneeda should not be confused with **Needmore**! This hamlet was named in the late 1800s for Uneeda brand crackers. As some tell it, when the name residents wanted was rejected, someone noticed a box of Uneeda crackers, and jokingly submitted Uneeda as the hamlet name!

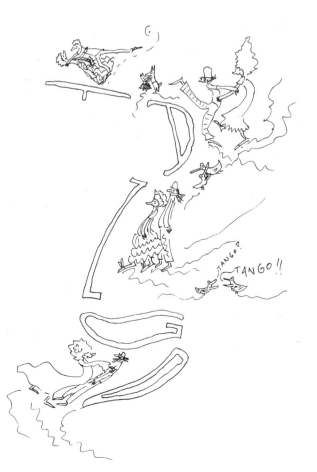

West Virginia

Southeastern State
35th State, Statehood 1863

Info to Know

Coal is used to generate electricity. In fact, it's the most commonly-used fuel for generating electricity in the United States. West Virginia is one of the largest coal producing states in the country. Almost every county in West Virginia (53 out of 55) has coal! Forty-three of them have coal that can be mined.

Lay of the Land

A long way away from Odd is Harpers Ferry, a town in West Virginia's extreme northeast, where the Potomac and Shenandoah Rivers meet. Harpers Ferry is known for its beauty and history. Among its many historical events, President George Washington chose it as the site for a United States armory and arsenal, where weapons were made and stored. In 1859, abolitionist John Brown raided the armory, in an unsuccessful attempt to start an armed rebellion to end slavery. Harpers Ferry was also the site of many Civil War battles, and of the largest surrender of Federal troops during the Civil War. There are many things to do in and around Harpers Ferry, including whitewater rafting on the Shenandoah and Potomac Rivers.

Road Trip

About 20 miles north of Odd is Beckley, southern West Virginia's largest city. It houses the Beckley Exhibition Mine, where you can ride an authentic coal car through a real underground coal mine! Tours are led by former miners. On the grounds you'll also find a reconstructed coal camp, which will help you get a sense of what life was like in the coal mining towns of the early 1900s.

No need to get all red in the face! **Embarrass** actually comes from a French word, *embarras*, meaning "obstacle" or "blockage." About a hundred years ago, northeastern Wisconsin, where this town is located, was filled with pine forests. Many of the pine trees were chopped down and sent down rivers to sawmills, where they were cut into timber. One river had so many snags and turns that the pine logs were constantly getting stuck. So the French-Canadian lumberjacks named it *Rivière Embarras*, meaning "Obstacle River" in French. The Americans called it the Embarrass River, and the town took its name from the river. And there's no shame in that!

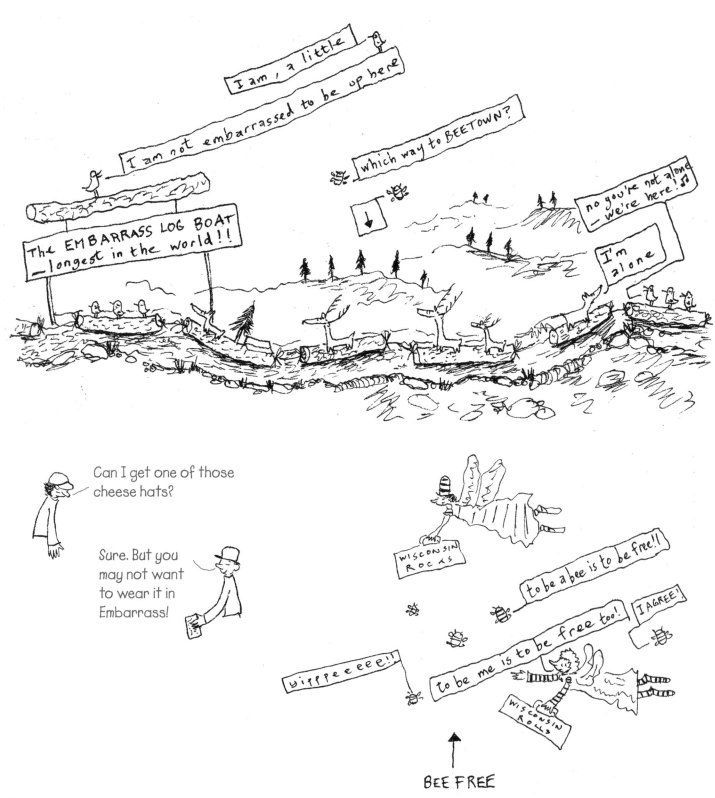

BEE FREE

Some Other Wacky Wisconsin Town Names:

Bear Trap	Fence
Beetown	Footville
Blueberry	Imalone
Cream	Luck
Eleva	Porcupine

In 1827, a man named Cyrus Alexander overturned a bee tree and found a huge nugget of lead. This lead became known as bee lead and the town, as **Beetown**.

Eleva might not be the funniest *sounding* name, but you'll love the reason behind it! A grain elevator had been built near the railroad tracks in the community of New Chicago, and a sign saying ELEVATOR was being painted. But winter set in before the sign was completed, and it was left saying ELEVA. When newcomers came to town, they saw the sign and thought Eleva was the community's name! It caught on, and New Chicago was renamed Eleva! (An alternative, but not as exciting, explanation is that the name was taken from a French village.)

Luck was named by Daniel F. Smith, who said he wanted be in luck for the rest of his life!

Wisconsin

Midwestern State
17th State, Statehood 1803

Info to Know

The Yellowstone Trail was the first highway in the United States that went across the country, from coast to coast. It stretched across the northern part of the United States and ran right through Wisconsin's Waupaca County, where Embarrass is located.

Lay of the Land

A popular vacation spot in the Midwest is the Dells of the Wisconsin River, also known as the Wisconsin Dells. It is a five-mile gorge on the Wisconsin River, in south central Wisconsin, with beautiful sandstone cliffs and rock formations, and narrow canyons. One way to tour the Wisconsin Dells is on a duck! Not the animal, but a vehicle originally designed for World War II, which travels on land and on water!

Road Trip

After you've enjoyed the natural wonders of the Wisconsin Dells, you can head over to the nearby city of Wisconsin Dells, which, along with the town of Lake Delton, houses a popular resort area. It has water parks, theme parks, water-ski shows, boat tours, golfing, mini-golf, go-carting, museums, and many other tourist attractions and activities!

And while you're in Wisconsin, make sure to attend a major sporting event, where you'll see fans wearing hats resembling wedges of cheese! That's because Wisconsin makes more cheese than any other state in the country, earning Wisconsinites the nickname Cheeseheads!

Hole-In-The-Wall is not actually a town: It's a valley that was once used as a hideout by outlaws of the Wild West, such as Butch Cassidy and the Sundance Kid! The hideout was called Hole-In-The-Wall because the only way in from the east was through a "hole in a wall," a narrow v-shaped gap in a wall of red rock cliffs about 50 miles long, often called the Red Wall. Aside from being hard to find and enter, the hideout was easy to defend, and a good lookout point for approaching lawmen. Hole-In-The-Wall was part of a chain of hideouts along a trail known as the Outlaw Trail. Around 1880-1890, about 30 to 40 outlaws spent time in Hole-In-The-Wall.

Some Other Wacky Wyoming Town Names:

Aladdin
Badwater
Bar Nunn
Bill
Burnt Fork
Chugwater
Cokeville
Dull Center
Dumbell
Goose Egg
Midwest
Recluse
Ten Sleep

TEN SLEEP, WYOMING

PIE-CRUST HILL

how many sleeps a bird got to go to get some more pie?

NO-PIE VALLEY

* approximately thirty one sleeps away from NO-PIE VALLEY average for any snail

Bill was so named because of all the ranchers in the area named Bill!

A *recluse* is someone who lives in solitude, avoiding contact with other people. The town of **Recluse** got its name either because its post office was far from the ranchers who used it, or because the community was in a remote location.

Some Indian tribes measured distance by how many days (sleeps) it would take to arrive at one's destination — how much distance one could cover between sleeps. The community of **Ten Sleep** was ten sleeps away from both Fort Laramie and Yellowstone Park. It was also ten sleeps from the Great Sioux Camps to the south, and from the northern camp, near Bridger, Montana.

EQUALITY
FREEDOM
WE HAVE THE RIGHT TO VOTE
hear hear!
WOMENS' RIGHTS
WE DESERVE TO VOTE

Wyoming was the first state to allow women to vote.

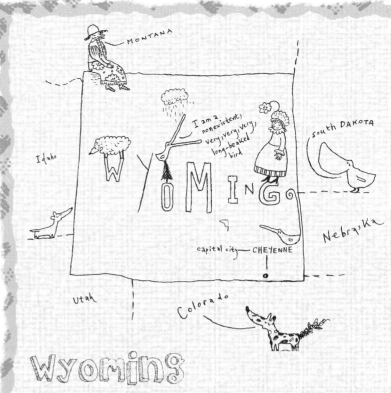

MONTANA

Idaho

I am a nonexistent, very, very, very long-beaked bird

WYOMING

South DAKOTA

Nebraska

capital city — CHEYENNE

Utah

Colorado

Wyoming

Western State
44th State, Statehood 1890

Info to Know

Wyoming was the first state to allow women to vote. Women were given the right to vote in Wyoming back in 1869, when it was still a territory. That's 51 years before the rest of the country.

Lay of the Land

A famous site in northeast Wyoming is Devil's Tower, a strange-looking geological formation of igneous rock that resembles a giant tree stump. It was the first national monument in the United States. It was also featured in Steven Spielberg's classic science fiction film, *Close Encounters of the Third Kind*. Another famous site in northwest Wyoming is Yellowstone National Park, the nation's first, largest, and most popular national park! Highlights include geysers like Old Faithful, mud pots, waterfalls, and The Grand Canyon of the Yellowstone.

Road Trip

The passage leading to Hole-In-The-Wall is on the property of Willow Creek Ranch, a 57,000-acre working ranch in central Wyoming and a guest ranch for vacationers! It's located at the southern end of the Big Horn Mountains and is surrounded on the east and south by the Red Wall. As sunlight changes throughout the day, the wall seems to change in color. There's lots to do at Willow Creek Ranch, including cattle driving, horseback riding through canyons, and taking a five-day Outlaw Trail ride, where you'll camp with an authentic chuck wagon!

★ WASHINGTON, D.C. ★

Capital of the United States
Founded July 16, 1790

Hey! Where's the funny-named town in *this* state? The answer is...nowhere! That's because Washington, D.C., is not a state at all! It's a city, and the capital of the whole country! Washington was named for—you guessed it—George Washington, the first president of the United States, and the one who chose this site as the nation's capital. "D.C." stands for *District of Columbia.* "District" means it's a federal district, a place that is designated as the seat of government, and that does not belong to any state. "Columbia" was named for Christopher Columbus. Washington, D.C., is located between Maryland and Virginia.

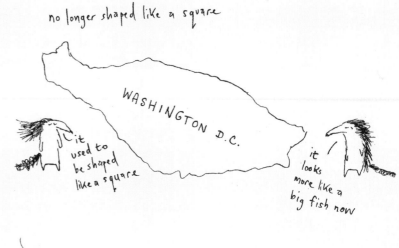

no longer shaped like a square

WASHINGTON D.C.

it used to be shaped like a square

it looks more like a big fish now

NEW YORK

where's Washington D.C.? I'm sure it was somewhere near here yesterday

I think it's moved to Philadelphia

EXTREMELY IMPORTANT BUILDING

— MONUMENT OF EXTREME POINTINESS

MUSEUM OF VERY IMPORTANT, OFFICIAL, GOVERNMENTY-TYPE THINGS

stars and strips fountain

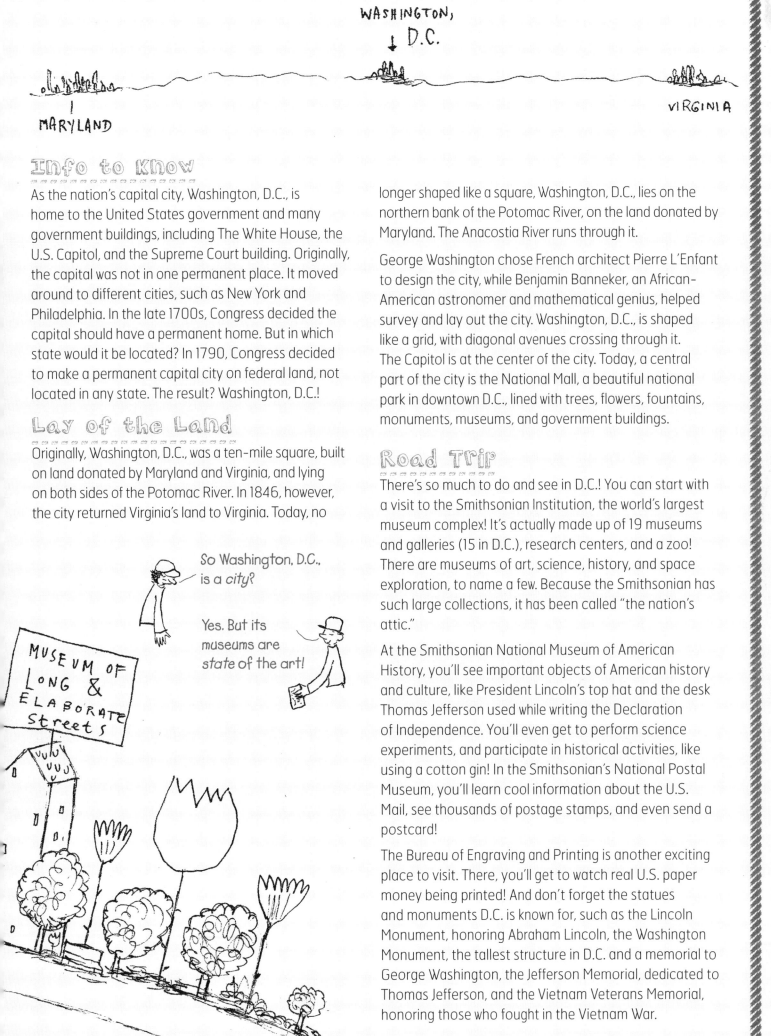

WASHINGTON, ↓ D.C.

MARYLAND

VIRGINIA

Info to Know

As the nation's capital city, Washington, D.C., is home to the United States government and many government buildings, including The White House, the U.S. Capitol, and the Supreme Court building. Originally, the capital was not in one permanent place. It moved around to different cities, such as New York and Philadelphia. In the late 1700s, Congress decided the capital should have a permanent home. But in which state would it be located? In 1790, Congress decided to make a permanent capital city on federal land, not located in any state. The result? Washington, D.C.!

Lay of the Land

Originally, Washington, D.C., was a ten-mile square, built on land donated by Maryland and Virginia, and lying on both sides of the Potomac River. In 1846, however, the city returned Virginia's land to Virginia. Today, no longer shaped like a square, Washington, D.C., lies on the northern bank of the Potomac River, on the land donated by Maryland. The Anacostia River runs through it.

George Washington chose French architect Pierre L'Enfant to design the city, while Benjamin Banneker, an African-American astronomer and mathematical genius, helped survey and lay out the city. Washington, D.C., is shaped like a grid, with diagonal avenues crossing through it. The Capitol is at the center of the city. Today, a central part of the city is the National Mall, a beautiful national park in downtown D.C., lined with trees, flowers, fountains, monuments, museums, and government buildings.

Road Trip

There's so much to do and see in D.C.! You can start with a visit to the Smithsonian Institution, the world's largest museum complex! It's actually made up of 19 museums and galleries (15 in D.C.), research centers, and a zoo! There are museums of art, science, history, and space exploration, to name a few. Because the Smithsonian has such large collections, it has been called "the nation's attic."

At the Smithsonian National Museum of American History, you'll see important objects of American history and culture, like President Lincoln's top hat and the desk Thomas Jefferson used while writing the Declaration of Independence. You'll even get to perform science experiments, and participate in historical activities, like using a cotton gin! In the Smithsonian's National Postal Museum, you'll learn cool information about the U.S. Mail, see thousands of postage stamps, and even send a postcard!

The Bureau of Engraving and Printing is another exciting place to visit. There, you'll get to watch real U.S. paper money being printed! And don't forget the statues and monuments D.C. is known for, such as the Lincoln Monument, honoring Abraham Lincoln, the Washington Monument, the tallest structure in D.C. and a memorial to George Washington, the Jefferson Memorial, dedicated to Thomas Jefferson, and the Vietnam Veterans Memorial, honoring those who fought in the Vietnam War.

So Washington, D.C., is a *city*?

Yes. But its museums are *state of the art!*

MUSEUM OF LONG & ELABORATE streets

Bibliography

Blevins, Don. *Peculiar, Uncertain, and Two Egg: The Unusual Origins of More Than 3,000 American Place Names*. Nashville: Cumberland House, 2000.

Bradfield, Bill and Bradfield, Clare. *Muleshoe and More: The Remarkable Stories Behind the Naming of Texas Towns*. Houston: Gulf Publishing Company, 1999.

Buller, Jon, et al. *Smart About the Fifty States*. New York: Grosset and Dunlap, 2003.

Davis, Kenneth C. *Don't Know Much About the 50 States*. New York: Harper Collins, 2001.

Doughty, Andrew. *Hawaii The Big Island Revealed: The Ultimate Guidebook*; 5th Ed. Lihu'e, Hawaii: Wizard Publications, 2008.

Gallant, Frank K. *A Place Called Peculiar: Stories About Unusual Place Names*: Springfield, MA: Merriam-Webster, 1998.

Gladstone, Gary. *Passing Gas and Other Towns Along the American Highway*. Berkeley: Ten Speed Press, 2003

Gladstone, Gary. *Reaching Climax and Other Towns Along the American Highway*. Berkeley: Ten Speed Press, 2006.

Insight Guides. *Hawaii*. London, England: Discovery Channel, APA Publications. 2008.

Jouris, David. *All Over the Map*. Berkeley: Ten Speed Press, 1994.

Jouris, David. *All Over the Map Again*. Berkeley: Ten Speed Press, 1996.

McMillen, Margot Ford. *Paris, Tightwad, and Peculiar: Missouri Place Names*. Columbia, MO: University of Missouri Press, 1994.

National Geographic United States Atlas for Young Explorers; 3rd Edition. Washington, D.C.: National Geographic, 2008.

Pizer, Vernon. *Ink, Ark., and All That: How American Places Got Their Names*. New York: G.P. Putnam's Sons, 1976.

Pukui, Mary Kawena, Elbert, Samuel H., and Mookini, Esther T. *Place Names of Hawaii*. Honolulu: University of Hawaii Press, 1974. Reprint, 1986.

Quimby, Myron J. *Scratch Ankle, U.S.A.: American Place Names and Their Derivation*. Cranbury, NJ: A.S. Barnes and Company, 1969. Reprint, 1970.

Stewart, George R. *American Place-Names: A Concise and Selective Dictionary for the Continental United States of America*. New York: Oxford University Press, 1985.

Usler, Mark. *Hometown Revelations: How America's Cities, Towns, and States Acquired Their Names*. Independence, MO: DM Enterprises, 2006.

Wichman, Frederick B. *Kaua'i Ancient Place-Names and Their Stories*. Honolulu: Univerity of Hawaii Press, 1998.

Wolk, Allan. *The Naming of America: How Continents, Countries, States, Counties, Cities, Towns, Villages, Hamlets, and Post Offices Came By Their Names*. Nashville:Thomas Nelson Inc., 1977.

Internet Sites:
Podunk.com
http://www.epodunk.com/

The Handbook of Texas Online: Texas State Historical Association
http://www.tshaonline.org/handbook/online/index.html

Acknowledgments

Thanks to the Kane Miller staff, and especially to my editor, Kira Lynn, for her interest, excitement and Confidence (CA) in the project, and her amazingly quick e-mail response time! Kira, it was a real Delight (NE) working with you!

On the road to researching and writing this book, I encountered many helpful people along the way:

Shelly Brown, Hawaiiana Reference Librarian, Hawaii State Library; Hawaii State Library, Hawaii & Pacific Section; Keli'i Brown, Director, Public Relations & Promotions, Maui Visitors and Convention Bureau; James Faczak, Naturalist for the NJ Division of Parks and Forestry, Cheesequake State Park; Lewis Johnson, Assistant Curator, Seminole Nation Museum, Wewoka, OK; David Ludlow, Executive Director of the Wilmington & Western Railroad; Deborah Mercer, New Jersey Collections Librarian, New Jersey State Library; Kitty Pittman, Administrative and Oklahoma Collection Librarian, Oklahoma Department of Libraries; Marta Ramey, Hamner Room Clerk, Briggs Library, OH; Carol Smythe, APHNYS Registered Historian, Town of Neversink, NY; Kaycee, Wyoming Chamber of Commerce; Willow Creek Ranch At The Hole-In-The-Wall; Michael Gross, Authors Guild; David Adler; Anna Olswanger; Lois Schnitzer; Ken Solin; Karen Reiffman (*Ink* consultant); David Becker (chozeh consultant); Dov Segal (blues consultant); Abby Carmel and Orlee Guttman (French consultants).

Thanks everyone! I am filled with Gratitude (MD)!

Debbie Herman